Inhalt

Vorwort

Was man von Oscar Wilde auch zitiert oder auswählt, immer wird es wie ein Fraktal seine ganze Biographie miterzählen. Und die war spektakulär genug – als Geschichte eines rapiden Aufstiegs zum Star- und Kultautor der »Yellow Nineties« und eines noch rasanteren Absturzes auf dem Höhepunkt des Ruhms, als Tragödie eines Komödienschreibers von Rang, als die über fünf Jahre zerdehnte soziale Exekution dieses genialen Aphoristikers, der mit traumwandlerischer Sicherheit ins Schwarze, ins Herz der viktorianischen Selbstgefälligkeit und Heuchelei getroffen hatte. Das ist der Stoff, aus dem die Mythen sind, und die Idolisierung Wildes ist im 20. Jahrhundert denn auch durch eine nicht abreißende Kette von Lebensbeschreibungen und -verfilmungen energisch vorangetrieben worden.

Aber Amüsement, möchte man meinen, steht doch wohl nur diesseits der existenziellen Katastrophe im Central Criminal Court, Old Bailey, und vor seiner Aburteilung wegen Homosexualität am 25. Mai 1895 zu erwarten, die den Dandy und Poseur in den Häftling C. 3. 3 verwandelte. Denn war das Rollenspiel und die Selbstinszenierung nicht sein Lebenselexier? Der junge Wilde hatte noch keine seiner erfolgreichen Gesellschaftskomödien geschrieben, war noch nicht als Essayist oder Verfasser des skandalumwitterten *Dorian Gray* hervorgetreten, da gab es ihn schon als öffentliche Person etwa in *Punch*- und *Vanity Fair*-Karikaturen, in der satirischen Operette *Patience* von Gilbert und Sullivan oder auf W. P. Friths Gemälde »The Private View of the Royal Academy in 1881«.

Doch Wilde war zu gewitzt, um eine bloße Witzfigur zu bleiben. Was andere für einen literarischen Fehlstart gehalten hätten, nutzte er konsequent als Karrieresprungbrett. War er anfangs in den Köpfen seiner Zeitgenossen nur als Verkörperung eines dekadenten und also lebensuntüchtigen Schönheitskults präsent gewesen, so erzeugte er jetzt systematisch jene Aura des Erfolgs um sich, die selbst einen Ästhetizisten gesellschaftsfähig machte, weil er (es) nun verdiente. Der Zweck heiligte dabei die Mittel. So kamen die fünf Auflagen von Wildes erstem Gedichtband dadurch zustande, dass man die Druckerpresse nach je 200 Exemplaren stoppte und dann wieder anfuhr. Die Lesereise durch die USA wurde erst in den Augen der von Wilde ausführlich ins Bild gesetzten Zurückgebliebenen triumphal, und auch die editorische Tätigkeit für die Frauenzeitschrift *Woman's World* profilierte mindestens zu gleichen Teilen das Periodikum und seinen Herausgeber.

Trotzdem geht dieser Fin-de-siècle-Autor in seinen Selbstvermarktungsstrategien nicht auf, darf man das Phänomen Wilde nicht auf rhetorische Pyrotechnik und eine augenzwinkernde Variante literarischer Hochstapelei reduzieren. Sicher, Wilde wusste aus dem Stand ein geistsprühendes Feuerwerk abzubrennen, von dem sein Zeitgenosse Frank Harris einmal bemerkte: »The extraordinary thing about Oscar's talent was that he did not monopolise the conversation. He took the ball of talk wherever it happened to be at the moment and played with it so humorously that everyone was soon smiling delightedly.« Aber er war deswegen noch lange kein Blender, der, um einen Vorwurf des Kritikers Arthur Symons zu reaktivieren, die

Pose des Weisen, des Poeten, des Künstlers gepflegt hätte, ohne auch nur eines davon wirklich zu sein.

»From a label there is no escape«, wehrt sich Lord Henry im *Dorian Gray* gegen die Automatismen des Zu- und Einordnens, gegen ein abstempelndes »nichts als«. Und entsprechend hat auch sein Schöpfer ein Faible für den Etikettenschwindel, für jenes blitzschnelle Auf-den-Kopf-Stellen und Austauschen von kategorischen Auf- und Überschriften, das im Reich der Werte Frivolität, auf dem Schachbrett der Logik Paradoxie heißt. Es kann folglich auch mit dem biographischen Auseinanderdividieren des einen Lebenswerks in die bis 1895 währende Phase effektzentrierter hedonistischer Sprachspiele und das sich anschließende »geläuterte« Endspiel von *De Profundis* oder der *Ballad of Reading Gaol* nicht seine Richtigkeit haben. Und die vorliegende Auswahl möchte vor allem ein Schuld-und-Sühne-Schema auflösen helfen, das die Arbeiten Wildes und ihre ganz eigentümliche Vergnüglichkeit so nachhaltig verfälscht.

Die lebensgeschichtliche Gegenläufigkeit des Vor-dem-Prozess und Nach-der-Verurteilung wird nämlich in den Texten selbst komplementär überbrückt. Was damit gemeint ist, erklärt man am besten mit Hilfe des von Wilde häufig verwendeten Doppelgängermotivs. Immer, von Anfang bis Ende, ist hinter dem, was sich bei ihm ostentativ in den Vordergrund spielt, ein Zweites, ein Schatten, ein Echo da. Der an den Pranger gestellte, ausgegrenzte, geächtete Wilde, der hoffnungslose Fall, redet so schon bei den rauschenden Erfolgen mit, und umgekehrt überlebt der Spötter und frivole Selbstdarsteller das Gefängnis oder wird zumindest in der Schäbigkeit des sich anschließenden Exils wieder-geboren. Der gefeierte und beklatschte Dramatiker wusste nur zu genau, was er mit seinen auf Hochglanz polierten Dialogen überspielte; der als Sebastian Melmoth immer wieder vor seinen Schulden davonreisende Ex-Sträfling begriff sich gleichwohl als »zany of sorrow«, als »clown whose heart is broken« und gab in seiner Korrespondenz die Bonmots weiterhin mit vollen Händen aus, geizte kaum jemals mit Selbstironie.

Wilde war auf die unterhaltsame Provokation, eine Heterodoxie ohne Bekehrungswut aus und hat auf seine unverwechselbare Art eine Lanze für die »philosophy of the superficial« gebrochen. Richtig gelesen bedeutet das, weder die Freiräume des spielerischen Unernstes preiszugeben noch ihn mit jenem dümmlichen Klamauk zu verwechseln, der heute von den Fernsehsendern als Sitcom in Serie produziert wird. Ein auf den ersten Blick ganz unaufwändiger Aphorismus wie »The basis of optimism is sheer terror« macht das deutlich. Geboren wohl aus der Lust am bloßen Auf-den-Kopf-Stellen des landläufigen Zusammendenkens von optimistischem Naturell, Weltvertrauen und Veränderungswillen – solche eher mechanische Inversionsaphoristik ist bei Wilde vielfach belegt –, tut sich im Einfall, beim lässigen Umstülpen, plötzlich ein Abgrund auf. Über dem Optimismus liegt nicht länger der warme Schimmer einer besseren Zukunft, die aufgrund wohl überlegter Entscheidungen »gemacht« wird; er erscheint jetzt im Flackerlicht als Panikreaktion von Überforderten, die mit der Einsicht in die eigene Ohnmacht nicht mehr zu Rande kommen. Wie durch einen Spalt, einen winzigen aphoristischen Sehschlitz, wird verbotenes philosophisches Terrain sichtbar, eine zutiefst dissidente antihegelianische, anticomtesche Geschichtsphilosophie, die Wilde u. a. in den *Intentions*-Dialogen weiter vorangetrieben hat. Und vielleicht macht schon dieses Einzelzitat deutlich, dass sich Thomas Mann mitnichten vergriff, als er »eine überraschende Familienähnlichkeit« zwischen Nietzsches Aperçus und Wildes »keineswegs nur eitlen Attacken« konstatierte und fortfuhr: »Die erste Form, in der der europäische Geist gegen die Gesamtmoral des bürgerlichen Zeitalters rebellierte, [war] der Ästhetizismus. Nicht umsonst habe ich Nietzsche und Wilde zusammen genannt – als Revoltierende, und zwar im Namen der Schönheit Revoltierende, gehören sie zusammen.«

Dieses Vergnügen, nein, dieser Höllenspaß an der bis in den Aberwitz, bis zum »Unverzeihlichen« getriebenen literarischen Revolte ist der gemeinsame Nenner des frühen, mittleren und exilierten Wilde, des Dramatikers, Essayisten und Briefeschreibers. »Antinomian spirit« nennt Wilde jenen Widerspruchsgeist, und es gibt in dieser kleinen Anthologie keine Seite, die nicht seinen Stempel trüge. Er ist es, der die Helden des Britischen Empire in Salonlöwen und parlierende Pappkameraden verwandelt, die vom Viktorianismus zu »angel[s] in the house« (C. Patmore) entrückten Frauen aber mit einem gerüttelt Maß an Realitätssinn und bisweilen fast raubtierhaftem Biss ausstattet. Er stiftet zu einem wahrheitsindifferenten Spiel mit Ideen und Werten an, das etwa die Natur ins Gefolge der sie vormals abbildenden und nachahmenden Kunst zwingt, sich andererseits aber die sprachlich gekonnten Landschaftsaquarelle, die impressionistischen »Ortstermine« nicht verbieten lässt. Er ist so frei, die moralische Keule zur Verteidigung eines »lasterhaften« Romans zu benutzen und sie seinen Kritikern fast gleichzeitig aus der Hand zu schlagen.

Wenn der Sinn des Lebens, wie Lord Illingworth in *A Woman of No Importance* einmal behauptet, darin besteht, »to be always looking for temptations«, dann war Wilde ein versucherischer Denker, und zwar im doppelten Wortsinn des Tentativen und des Verführerischen. Deshalb sind seine (Selbst-) Widersprüche immer heuristisch, seine Paradoxien nie inkonsequent. Sein Kopf war das, was man in der Teilchenphysik einen »Collider« nennt, will sagen, er ließ darin Überzeugungen, Theoreme, Ideen, letzte und vorletzte Wahrheiten aufeinanderprallen, um den elementaren Kräften auf die Spur zu kommen, die unsere Wirklichkeit zusammenhalten.

Als sein großes Lebensexperiment im Kreuzverhör der Anklage entgleiste und man ihn als »Perversen« finanziell in den Bankrott, literarisch in die Unles- bzw. Unspielbarkeit getrieben hatte, war auch nach zwei Jahren Einzelhaft noch so viel von dem alten Antinomiker übrig, dass er sich den falschen Tröstungen des Selbstmitleids verschließen und zum letzten Mal aus einer ihm von außen zudiktierten Rolle schlüpfen konnte: der des Märtyrers. Seine künstlerische Existenz lag nämlich gar nicht in Trümmern, sondern war – in bester Wildescher Paradoxie – gerade durch den irreparablen Bruch ganz geworden und zur Vollendung gelangt. Und eben das war es, was ihn am Grab seiner Frau nicht minder tief bewegte als ihr früher Tod: jener »sense of the uselessness of all regrets«, der nur die pietätvolle Verkleidung der Gewissheit darstellt, dass ein Leben in seinen Höhen und Tiefen, seinen Leistungen, Torheiten und seiner Schuld richtig war und ganz so geglückt, wie auch ein Kunstwerk geglückt und aus einem Guss sein muss.

Trotzdem wird Wilde nie monumental werden. Dazu hat er zu unermüdlich gegen alles Imposante, alles in Ehrfurcht vor sich selbst Erstarrte angeschrieben. Ein Denkmal, insbesondere ein Denkmal des »Opfers« Wilde, wäre also auch nach seinem hundertsten Todestag unangebracht. Wer ihn ehren will, nimmt so eine Installation lieber beim Wort, denkt nicht nur einmal, sondern möglichst oft und dann auch noch mit Wildes Lieblingsautor Huysmans »à rebours«, gegen den Strich. Und wem das nicht genügt, der wiederhole die Geste Robert Ross' vor dem Konkursgericht, die Wilde »in the treasury-house of [his] heart« aufbewahrte, und ziehe den Hut.

I

Prince Paradox or How to Pose on a Pedestal

"His name is Prince Paradox," said Dorian.

"I recognise him in a flash," exclaimed the Duchess.

"I won't hear of it," laughed Lord Henry, sinking into a chair. "From a label there is no escape! I refuse the title."

"Royalties may not abdicate," fell as a warning from pretty lips.

"You wish me to defend my throne, then?"

"Yes."

"I give the truths of to-morrow."

"I prefer the mistakes of to-day," she answered.

"You disarm me, Gladys," he cried, catching the wilfulness of her mood.

"Of your shield, Harry: not of your spear."

"I never tilt against beauty," he said, with a wave of his hand.

5 **in a flash:** im Nu, sofort.
Duchess: Herzogin.
7 **label:** Etikett.
9 **royalty:** Mitglied der königlichen Familie.
to abdicate: abdanken.
15 **to disarm** (fig.): entwaffnen.
15f. **wilfulness:** Halsstarrigkeit, Eigensinn.
18 **to tilt against s.th.:** gegen etwas zu Felde ziehen.

Oscar Wilde photographed by Napoleon Sarony, 1882

"That is your error, Harry, believe me. You value beauty far too much."

"How can you say that? I admit that I think that it is better to be beautiful than to be good. But on the other hand no one is more ready than I am to acknowledge that it is better to be good than to be ugly."

"Ugliness is one of the seven deadly sins, then?" cried the Duchess. "What becomes of your simile about the orchid?"

"Ugliness is one of the seven deadly virtues, Gladys. You, as a good Tory, must not underrate them. Beer, the Bible, and the seven deadly virtues have made our England what she is."

"You don't like your country, then?" she asked.

"I live in it."

"That you may censure it the better."

"Would you have me take the verdict of Europe on it?" he inquired.

"What do they say of us?"

"That Tartuffe has emigrated to England and opened a shop."

"Is that yours, Harry?"

"I give it to you."

"I could not use it. It is too true."

"You need not be afraid. Our countrymen never recognise a description."

8 **simile:** Vergleich.
9 **orchid:** Orchidee.
11 **Tory:** Anhänger der konservativen Partei Großbritanniens.
to underrate: unterschätzen.
16 **to censure:** kritisieren, tadeln.
17 **verdict:** Urteil.
20 **Tartuffe:** Heuchler in Molières gleichnamiger Komödie (1664).

"They are practical."

"They are more cunning than practical. When they make up their ledger, they balance stupidity by wealth, and vice by hypocrisy."

"Still, we have done great things."

"Great things have been thrust on us, Gladys."

"We have carried their burden."

"Only as far as the Stock Exchange."

She shook her head. "I believe in the race," she cried.

"It represents the survival of the pushing."

"It has development."

"Decay fascinates me more."

"What of Art?" she asked.

"It is a malady."

"Love?"

"An illusion."

"Religion?"

"The fashionable substitute for Belief."

"You are a sceptic."

"Never! Scepticism is the beginning of Faith."

"What are you?"

"To define is to limit."

"Give me a clue."

"Threads snap. You would lose your way in the labyrinth."

The Picture of Dorian Gray; CW 147–148

2 **cunning:** schlau, verschlagen.
3 **to make up the ledger:** Buch führen.
to balance aufrechnen, ausgleichen.
4 **hypocrisy:** Heuchelei.
6 **to thrust s.th. on s.o.:** jdm. etwas auferlegen.
8 **Stock Exchange:** Londoner Börse.
14 **malady:** (schleichende) Krankheit.
24 **to snap:** (zer)reißen.

I live in terror of not being misunderstood. Don't degrade me into the position of giving you useful information. CW 1016

It is only the intellectually lost who ever argue. CW 25

I choose my friends for their good looks, my acquaintances for their characters, and my enemies for their brains. CW 23

A man who can dominate a London dinner-table can dominate the world. The future belongs to the dandy. It is the exquisites who are going to rule. CW 459

A really well-made buttonhole is the only link between art and nature. CW 1205

There is no such thing as a moral or an immoral book. Books are well written, or badly written. That is all. CW 17

When critics disagree the artist is in accord with himself. CW 17

The more one analyses people, the more all reasons for analysis disappear. Sooner or later one comes to that dreadful universal thing called human nature. Indeed, as any one who has ever worked among the poor

2 **to degrade s.o. into s.th.:** jdn. zu etwas erniedrigen, herabwürdigen.
10 **exquisite:** feinsinniger Mensch, Dandy.
11 **buttonhole:** Blume im Knopfloch.
16 **to be in accord:** im Einklang stehen, sich im Einklang befinden.

knows only too well, the brotherhood of man is no mere poet's dream, it is a most depressing and humiliating reality. CW 975

The amount of women in London flirting with their own husbands is perfectly scandalous. It looks so bad. It is simply washing one's clean linen in public. CW 327

Ignorance is like a delicate exotic fruit; touch it and the bloom is gone. The whole theory of modern education is radically unsound. Fortunately in England, at any rate, education produces no effect whatsoever. If it did, it would prove a serious danger to the upper classes, and probably lead to acts of violence in Grosvenor Square. CW 332

Wickedness is a myth invented by good people to account for the curious attractiveness of others. CW 1205

Ambition is the last refuge of the failure. CW 1205

2f. **humiliating:** demütigend, beschämend.
6 **linen:** Wäsche.
7 **delicate:** zart, empfindlich.
8 **bloom:** Frische.
9 **unsound:** zweifelhaft.
12f. **Grosvenor Square:** Platz im vornehmen Londoner Stadtteil Mayfair.
14 **wickedness:** Verdorbenheit.
myth: Mythos, Gerücht.
14f. **to account for s.th.:** etwas begründen.
16 **refuge:** Zuflucht.

In this world, there are only two tragedies. One is not getting what one wants, and the other is getting it. The last is much the worst. CW 417

Poets know how useful passion is for publication. Nowadays a broken heart will run to many editions. CW 25

America is a paradise for women – that is why, like Eve, the American women are extremely anxious to get out of it. CW 436

If a woman wants to hold a man, she has merely to appeal to what is worst in him. We make gods of the men and they leave us. Others make brutes of them and they fawn and are faithful. CW 410

The only way to get rid of a temptation is to yield to it. CW 29

Twenty years of romance make a woman look like a ruin; but twenty years of marriage make her something like a public building. CW 440

One can survive everything nowadays, except death, and live down anything except a good reputation. CW 442

5 **to run to s.th.:** für etwas ausreichen.
7f. **to be anxious to do s.th.:** versessen darauf sein, etwas zu tun.
11 **brute:** Rohling.
12 **to fawn:** herumscharwenzeln.
13 **to yield to s.th.:** einer Sache nachgeben.
19 **to live down s.th.:** etwas hinter sich bringen.

The modern sympathy with invalids is morbid. Illness of any kind is hardly a thing to be encouraged in others. CW 329

The only difference between the saint and the sinner is that every saint has a past, and every sinner a future. CW 462

Prayer must never be answered: if it is, it ceases to be prayer and becomes conversation. WaH 106

It is well for his peace that the saint goes to his martyrdom. He is spared the sight of the horror of the harvest. CW 1024

Missionaries, my dear! Don't you realise that missionaries are the divinely provided food for destitute and underfed cannibals? Whenever they are on the brink of starvation, Heaven in its infinite mercy sends them a nice plump missionary. WaH 108

Society often forgives the criminal; it never forgives the dreamer. CW 1039

1 **morbid:** krankhaft, entartet.
9f. **martyrdom:** Martyrium.
10f. **harvest** (fig.): Ernte.
13 **divinely** (adv.): göttlich, himmlisch.
destitute: Not leidend.
14f. **to be on the brink of s.th.:** am Rande von etwas, kurz vor etwas stehen.
15 **starvation:** Hungertod.
16 **plump:** wohlgenährt.

I am a dreamer. For a dreamer is one who can only find his way by moonlight, and his punishment is that he sees the dawn before the rest of the world. CW 1058

As one reads history one is absolutely sickened, not by the crimes that the wicked have committed, but by the punishments that the good have inflicted; and a community is infinitely more brutalised by the habitual employment of punishment than it is by the occasional occurrence of crime. WaH 197

The basis of optimism is sheer terror. CW 67

We are all in the gutter, but some of us are looking at the stars. CW 417

Most people become bankrupt through having invested too heavily in the prose of life. To have ruined oneself over poetry is an honour. CW 52

Only mediocrities progress. An artist revolves in a cycle of masterpieces, the first of which is no less perfect than the last. WaH 61

Art is the only serious thing in the world. And the artist is the only person who is never serious. CW 1203

4 **to be sickened:** sich angeekelt fühlen.
6 **to inflict a punishment:** eine Strafe verhängen.
7 **habitual:** gewohnheitsmäßig.
10 **sheer:** rein, schier.
11 **gutter:** Gosse.
14 **prose of life:** Alltäglichkeit.
16 **mediocrity:** Mittelmäßigkeit.
to revolve: sich drehen, kreisen.

It is absurd to have a hard and fast rule about what one should read and what one shouldn't. More than half of modern culture depends on what one shouldn't read. CW 324

The fact of a man being a poisoner is nothing against his prose. CW 1007

The only way to atone for being occasionally a little over-dressed is by being always absolutely over-educated. CW 1205

There are two ways of disliking art. One is to dislike it. The other is to like it rationally. CW 1047

A subject that is beautiful in itself gives no suggestion to the artist. It lacks imperfection. CW 1203

One should either be a work of art, or wear a work of art. CW 1206

Philosophy may teach us to bear with equanimity the misfortunes of our neighbours, and science resolve the moral sense into a secretion of sugar, but art is what makes the life of each citizen a sacrament. WaH 61

1 **a hard and fast rule:** eine verbindliche Regel.
6 **prose:** Prosastil.
7 **to atone for s.th.:** etwas wieder gut machen.
13 **imperfection:** Unvollkommenheit.
16 **equanimity:** Gleichmut, Gelassenheit.
17 **to resolve:** auflösen.
18 **secretion:** Sekret, Absonderung.

Style largely depends on the way the chin is worn. They are worn very high, just at present. CW 374

One should never listen. To listen is a sign of indifference to one's hearers. CW 1204

Only people who look dull ever get into the House of Commons, and only people who are dull ever succeed there. CW 539

Public opinion exists only where there are no ideas. CW 1203

The mind of a thoroughly well-informed man is like a bric-à-brac shop, all monsters and dust and everything priced above its proper value. CW 25

When we have fully discovered the scientific laws that govern life, we shall realise that the one person who has more illusions than the dreamer is the man of action. CW 1023

Science can never grapple with the irrational. That is why it has no future before it, in this world. CW 487

I can stand brute force, but brute reason is quite unbearable. There is something unfair about its use. It is hitting below the intellect. CW 43

3f. **indifference:** Gleichgültigkeit.
5f. **House of Commons:** Unterhaus (im britischen Parlament).
10 **bric-à-brac shop:** Antiquitätengeschäft.
16 **to grapple with s.th.:** etwas in den Griff bekommen.
18 **brute:** grob, roh.
18f. **to be unbearable:** unerträglich sein.

Humanity takes itself too seriously. It is the world's original sin. If the cavemen had known how to laugh, History would have been different. CW 44

To test Reality we must see it on the tight-rope. When the Verities become acrobats we can judge them. CW 43

One is tempted to define man as a rational animal who always loses his temper when he is called upon to act in accordance with the dictates of reason. CW 1044

The worst thing you can do for a person of genius is to help him: that way lies his destruction. I have many devoted helpers – and you see the result. WaH 203

It is sad. One half of the world does not believe in God, and the other half does not believe in me. WaH 249

The well-bred contradict other people. The wise contradict themselves. CW 1205

2 **original sin:** Erbsünde.
caveman: Höhlenmensch.
4 **tight-rope:** Hochseil.
5 **verity:** Wahrheit.
7 **to be called upon to do s.th.:** dazu aufgefordert sein, etwas zu tun.
8 **accordance:** Übereinstimmung.
dictates of reason: Gebote der Vernunft.
10f. **devoted:** ergeben, treu.
14 **well-bred:** wohlerzogen.

He played with the idea, and grew wilful; tossed it into the air and transformed it; let it escape and recaptured it; made it iridescent with fancy, and winged it with paradox. The praise of folly, as he went on, soared into a philosophy, and Philosophy herself became young, and catching the mad music of Pleasure, wearing, one might fancy, her wine-stained robe and wreath of ivy, danced like a Bacchante over the hills of life, and mocked the slow Silenus for being sober. Facts fled before her like frightened forest things. Her white feet trod the huge press at which wise Omar sits, till the seething grape-juice rose round her bare limbs in waves of purple bubbles, or crawled in red foam over the vat's back, dripping, sloping sides. It was an extraordinary improvisation. He felt that the eyes of Dorian

1 **wilful:** eigensinnig.
to toss: hochwerfen.
3 **iridescent:** schillernd, bunt.
to wing: beflügeln.
4 **folly:** Narrheit, Torheit.
to soar: aufsteigen, sich erheben.
7 **wine-stained:** mit Wein befleckt.
robe: Gewand.
wreath of ivy: Efeukranz.
8 **Bacchante:** Teilnehmerin am orgiastischen Kult des griechischen Weingottes Dionysos.
9 **to mock:** verspotten.
Silenus: Mischwesen aus Pferd und Mensch; Begleiter des Dionysos.
11 **to tread:** treten, stampfen.
press: Fruchtpresse, Kelter.
Omar: O. Chajjam, persischer Dichter, Mathematiker und Astronom (12. Jh.).
12 **seething:** schäumend.
13 **purple:** violett.
14 **vat:** Fass.

Gray were fixed on him, and the consciousness that amongst his audience there was one whose temperament he wished to fascinate, seemed to give his wit keenness, and to lend colour to his imagination. He was brilliant, fantastic, irresponsible. He charmed his listeners out of themselves, and they followed his pipe laughing. *The Picture of Dorian Gray*; CW 45

4 **keenness:** Schärfe.
5f. **to charm s.o. out of himself, herself:** jdn. verzaubern.

II

Joining the Lounge Lizards

ALGERNON *(inspects [the sandwiches], takes two, and sits down on the sofa)*. Oh! ... by the way, Lane, I see from your book that on Thursday night, when Lord Shoreman and Mr. Worthing were dining with me, eight bottles of champagne are entered as having been consumed.

LANE. Yes, sir; eight bottles and a pint.

ALGERNON. Why is it that at a bachelor's establishment the servants invariably drink the champagne? I ask merely for information.

LANE. I attribute it to the superior quality of the wine, sir. I have often observed that in married households the champagne is rarely of a first-rate brand.

ALGERNON. Good heavens! Is marriage so demoralising as that?

LANE. I believe it *is* a very pleasant state, sir. I have had very little experience of it myself up to the present. I have only been married once. That was in consequence of a misunderstanding between myself and a young person.

ALGERNON *(languidly)*. I don't know that I am much interested in your family life, Lane.

11 **invariably** (adv.): unweigerlich, ausnahmslos.
23 **languidly** (adv.): gelangweilt.

LANE. No, sir; it is not a very interesting subject. I never think of it myself.

ALGERNON. Very natural, I am sure. That will do, Lane, thank you.

LANE. Thank you, sir. *(Lane moves to go out.)*

ALGERNON. Ah! ... just give me another cucumber sandwich.

LANE. Yes, sir. *(Returns and hands plate.)*

(Lane goes out.)

ALGERNON. Lane's views on marriage seem somewhat lax. Really, if the lower orders don't set us a good example, what on earth is the use of them? They seem, as a class, to have absolutely no sense of moral responsibility. *The Importance of Being Earnest*; CW 321–322

The son, who had been his father's secretary, had resigned along with his chief, somewhat foolishly as was thought at the time, and on succeeding some months later to the title, had set himself to the serious study of the great aristocratic art of doing absolutely nothing. He had two large town houses, but preferred to live in chambers, as it was less trouble, and took most of his meals at his club. He paid some attention to the management of his collieries in the Midland counties, excusing himself for this taint of industry on the ground

6 **cucumber:** Gurke.
11 **lax:** nachlässig.
11f. **to set s.o. an example:** jdm. ein Beispiel geben.
20f. **in chambers:** möbliert.
23 **colliery:** Kohlenzeche.
24 **taint of industry:** Anflug von Betriebsamkeit.

Wilde during his first year at Oxford, 1875

that the one advantage of having coal was that it enabled a gentleman to afford the decency of burning wood on his own hearth. In politics he was a Tory, except when the Tories were in office, during which period he roundly abused them for being a pack of Radicals. He was a hero to his valet, who bullied him, and a terror to most of his relations, whom he bullied in turn. Only England could have produced him, and he always said that the country was going to the dogs. His principles were out of date, but there was a good deal to be said for his prejudices.

The Picture of Dorian Gray; CW 38

To an Income-tax Inspector

[? April 1889]

Sir, It was arranged last year that I should send in my income-tax return from Chelsea where I reside, as I am resigning my position here and will not be with Messrs Cassell after August. I think it would be better to continue that arrangement. I wish your notices were not so

2 **decency:** Anstand.
3 **hearth:** Herd.
Tory: Mitglied der konservativen Partei Großbritanniens.
4 **to be in office:** amtieren (Regierung).
5 **to abuse:** beschimpfen.
6 **valet:** (Kammer-)Diener.
to bully: schikanieren.
9 **to go to the dogs:** vor die Hunde gehen.
16 **income-tax return:** Steuererklärung.
Chelsea: Stadtteil von London.

agitating and did not hold out such dreadful threats. A penalty of fifty pounds sounds like a relic of mediaeval torture. Your obedient servant OSCAR WILDE

TL 242

There is no country in the world so much in need of unpractical people as this country of ours. With us, Thought is degraded by its constant association with practice. Who that moves in the stress and turmoil of actual existence, noisy politician, or brawling social reformer, or poor narrow-minded priest blinded by the sufferings of that unimportant section of the community among whom he has cast his lot, can seriously claim to be able to form a disinterested intellectual judgment about any one thing? Each of the professions means a prejudice. The necessity for a career forces every one to take sides. We live in the age of the overworked, and the under-educated; the age in which people are so industrious that they become absolutely stupid. And, harsh though it may sound, I cannot help

1 **agitating:** beunruhigend.
2 **relic:** Relikt, Überrest.
mediaeval: mittelalterlich.
8 **turmoil:** Gedränge, Tumult.
9 **to brawl:** brüllen, lärmen.
10 **narrow-minded:** engstirnig.
12 **to cast one's lot among s.o.:** das Los mit jdm. teilen.
16 **to take sides:** Partei ergreifen.
18 **industrious:** fleißig.
19 **harsh:** hart, grausam.

saying that such people deserve their doom. The sure way of knowing nothing about life is to try to make oneself useful. *The Critic as Artist;* CW 1042

To George Alexander

[February 1895] St James's Theatre

Dear Aleck, I am much obliged to you for your cheque for £ 300.

If it is possible could you let me have the balance as soon as possible. I am already served with writs for £ 400, rumours of prosperity having reached the commercial classes, and my hotel is loathsome to me. I want to leave it. TL 383

To the Editor of the Daily Telegraph

2 February 1891 London

Sir, With reference to the interesting article on men's dress and the fashions for next season that appears in today's ıssue of your paper, will you allow me to point out that the costume worn now by Mr Wyndham in

1 **doom:** Schicksal, Los.
8 **balance:** restlicher Betrag.
9 **writ:** Zahlungsbescheid.
11 **to be loathsome to s.o.:** jdm. verhasst sein.
15 **with reference to:** in Bezugnahme auf.
17 **issue:** Ausgabe (einer Zeitung).

London Assurance might be taken as the basis for a new departure, not in the style, but in the colour of modern evening dress. The costume in question belongs to 1840 or 1841, and its charm resides in the fact that the choice of the colour of the coat is left to the taste and fancy and inclination of the wearer. Freedom in such selection of colour is a necessary condition of variety and individualism of costume, and the uniform black that is worn now, though valuable at a dinner-party, where it serves to isolate and separate women's dresses, to frame them as it were, still is dull and tedious and depressing in itself, and makes the aspect of club-life and men's dinners monotonous and uninteresting. The little note of individualism that makes dress delightful can only be attained nowadays by the colour and treatment of the flower one wears. This is a great pity.

[…]

The coat, then, of next season, will be an exquisite colour-note, and have also a great psychological value. It will emphasise the serious and thoughtful side of a man's character. One will be able to discern a man's views of life by the colour he selects. The colour of the coat will be symbolic. It will be part of the wonderful symbolistic movement in modern art. The imagination will concentrate itself on the waistcoat. Waistcoats will

11 **to frame:** einrahmen.
11f. **tedious:** langweilig.
15 **to attain s.th.:** etwas erreichen, erzielen.
20 **colour-note:** Farbgebung.
22 **to discern:** erkennen.
26 **waistcoat:** Weste.

show whether a man can admire poetry or not. That will be very valuable. Over the shirt-front Fancy will preside. By a single glance one will be able to detect the tedious. TL 283–284

LORD ILLINGWORTH. […] [T]o be modern is the only thing worth being nowadays. You want to be modern, don't you, Gerald? You want to know life as it really is. Not to be put off with any old-fashioned theories about life. Well, what you have to do at present is simply to fit yourself for the best society. A man who can dominate a London dinner-table can dominate the world. The future belongs to the dandy. It is the exquisites who are going to rule.

GERALD. I should like to wear nice things awfully, but I have always been told that a man should not think so much about his clothes.

LORD ILLINGWORTH. People nowadays are so absolutely superficial that they don't understand the philosophy of the superficial. By the way, Gerald, you should learn how to tie your tie better. Sentiment is all very well for the buttonhole. But the essential thing for a necktie is style. A well-tied tie is the first serious step in life.

GERALD *(laughing)*. I might be able to learn how to tie

3 **to preside over s.th.:** etwas bestimmen.
8 **to be put off with s.th.:** mit etwas abgespeist werden.
13 **exquisite:** feinsinniger Mensch, Dandy.
18 **superficial:** oberflächlich.
21 **buttonhole:** Blume im Knopfloch.

a tie. Lord Illingworth, but I should never be able to talk as you do. I don't know how to talk.

LORD ILLINGWORTH. Oh! talk to every woman as if you loved her, and to every man as if he bored you, and at the end of your first season you will have the reputation of possessing the most perfect social tact.

GERALD. But it is very difficult to get into society, isn't it?

LORD ILLINGWORTH. To get into the best society, nowadays, one has either to feed people, amuse people, or shock people – that is all!

GERALD. I suppose society is wonderfully delightful!

LORD ILLINGWORTH. To be in it is merely a bore. But to be out of it simply a tragedy. Society is a necessary thing. No man has any real success in this world unless he has got women to back him, and women rule society. If you have not got women on your side you are quite over. You might just as well be a barrister or a stockbroker, or a journalist at once.

GERALD. It is very difficult to understand women, is it not?

LORD ILLINGWORTH. You should never try to understand them. Women are pictures. Men are problems. If you want to know what a woman really means – which, by the way, is always a dangerous thing to do – look at her, don't listen to her.

A Woman of No Importance; CW 459–460

18 **to be over:** verloren sein.
barrister: (plädierender) Rechtsanwalt.
19 **stockbroker:** Aktien-, Effektenhändler.

To More Adey

6 May 1897 H.M. Prison, Reading

My dear More, Many thanks for your letter.

[...]

As regards clothes etc: Robbie kindly said he would get me a blue-serge suit from Doré and an ulster: this I suppose he has done. Frank Harris also offered me some kindnesses of the same kind, so I have already written to him to say what I want in the way of other clothes, *and boots*, and to ask for the things to be sent to you, not later than Thursday 13th. Hats I ought to have a lot of, but I suppose they have disappeared: Heath, Albert Gate, was my hatter, and understands my needs: I would like a brown hat, and a grey hat, soft felt, seaside things. Would you, if there is time, get me *eighteen* collars made after the pattern you have, or say two dozen. Also, order me two dozen white handkerchiefs, and a dozen with coloured borders. Also some neckties: some dark blue with white spots and diapers, and some of whatever is being worn for summer wear. I also want eight pair of socks, coloured summer things; my size in gloves is 8¼, as my hand is so broad, but my socks need only be for an 8 glove in proportion. Also, I want two or three sets of plain mother-of-pearl (by the way I want to make "nacred"

5 **as regards:** betreffend.
6 **blue-serge:** aus blauem Serge (Gewebe).
ulster: Mantel.
15 **felt:** Filz.
19f. **spots and diapers:** Tupfen- und Rautenmuster.
25 **mother-of-pearl:** Perlmutt.
nacred: mit Perlmutt besetzt.

an English word) studs – nacred studs: you know how difficult they are to get abroad. Also, some nice French soap, Houbigant's if you can get it: Pritchard of King Street, St James's, used to have it for me: either "Peau d'Espagne" or "Sac de Laitue" would do: a case of three. Also, some scent; Canterbury Wood Violet I would like, and some "Eau de Lubin" for the toilet, a large bottle. Also some of Pritchard's tooth-powder, and a medium toothbrush. My hair has become very grey: I am under the impression that it is quite white, but I believe that is an exaggeration: there is a wonderful thing called Koko Marikopas, to be got at 233 Regent Street, which is a wonderful hair-tonic: the name alone seems worth the money, so please get a large bottle. I want, for psychological reasons, to feel entirely physically cleansed of the stain and soil of prison life, so these things are all – trivial as they may sound – really of great importance. TL 534–535

CECIL GRAHAM. Oh! gossip is charming! History is merely gossip. But scandal is gossip made tedious by morality. Now, I never moralise. A man who moralises is usually a hypocrite, and a woman who moralises is invariably plain. There is nothing in the whole

1 **studs:** Manschettenknöpfe.
6 **scent:** Parfüm.
16 **soil:** Schmutz, Dreck.
20 **tedious:** langweilig.
22 **hypocrite:** Heuchler.
23 **invariably** (adv.): unweigerlich.
plain: gewöhnlich.

world so unbecoming to a woman as a Nonconformist conscience. And most women know it, I'm glad to say.

LORD AUGUSTUS. Just my sentiments, dear boy, just my sentiments.

CECIL GRAHAM. Sorry to hear it, Tuppy; whenever people agree with me, I always feel I must be wrong.

LORD AUGUSTUS. My dear boy, when I was your age –

CECIL GRAHAM. But you never were, Tuppy, and you never will be. *(Goes up to C.)* I say, Darlington, let us have some cards. You'll play, Arthur, won't you?

LORD WINDERMERE. No, thanks, Cecil.

DUMBY *(with a sigh)*. Good heavens! how marriage ruins a man! It's as demoralising as cigarettes, and far more expensive.

CECIL GRAHAM. You'll play, of course, Tuppy?

LORD AUGUSTUS *(pouring himself out a brandy and soda at table)*. Can't, dear boy. Promised Mrs. Erlynne never to play or drink again.

CECIL GRAHAM. Now, my dear Tuppy, don't be led astray into the paths of virtue. Reformed, you would be perfectly tedious. That is the worst of women. They always want one to be good. And if we are good, when they meet us, they don't love us at all. They like to find us quite irretrievably bad, and to leave us quite unattractively good.

1 **unbecoming:** unkleidsam, unpassend.
1f. **Nonconformist:** protestantisch-freikirchlich.
4 **just my sentiments:** ganz Deiner Meinung.
10 **C.:** Abk. für *Central, Centre*.
20f. **to be led astray:** vom rechten Weg abgebracht werden.
25 **irretrievably** (adv.): unrettbar.

LORD DARLINGTON *(rising from R. Table, where he has been writing letters)*. They always do find us bad!

DUMBY. I don't think we are bad. I think we are all good, except Tuppy.

[…]

How long could you love a woman who didn't love you, Cecil?

CECIL GRAHAM. A woman who didn't love me? Oh, all my life!

DUMBY. So could I. But it's so difficult to meet one.

LORD DARLINGTON. How can you be so conceited, Dumby?

DUMBY. I didn't say it as a matter of conceit. I said it as a matter of regret. I have been wildly, madly adored. I am sorry I have. It has been an immense nuisance. I should like to be allowed a little time to myself now and then.

LORD AUGUSTUS (*looking round*). Time to educate yourself, I suppose.

DUMBY. No, time to forget all I have learned. That is much more important, dear Tuppy.

(Lord Augustus moves uneasily in his chair.)

LORD DARLINGTON. What cynics you fellows are!

CECIL GRAHAM. What is a cynic? *(Sitting on the back of the sofa.)*

LORD DARLINGTON. A man who knows the price of everything and the value of nothing.

CECIL GRAHAM. And a sentimentalist, my dear Darling-

1 **R.:** Abk. für *Right*.
11 **conceited:** eingebildet.
14 **to adore s.o.:** jdn. verehren, anbeten.
22 **uneasily** (adv.): unbehaglich, verlegen.

ton, is a man who sees an absurd value in everything, and doesn't know the market price of any single thing.

LORD DARLINGTON. You always amuse me, Cecil. You talk as if you were a man of experience.

CECIL GRAHAM. I am. *(Moves up to front of fireplace.)*

LORD DARLINGTON. You are far too young!

CECIL GRAHAM. That is a great error. Experience is a question of instinct about life. I have got it. Tuppy hasn't. Experience is the name Tuppy gives to his mistakes. That is all.

(Lord Augustus looks round indignantly.)

DUMBY. Experience is the name every one gives to their mistakes.

CECIL GRAHAM *(standing with his back to the fireplace)*. One shouldn't commit any.

Lady Windermere's Fan; CW 416–418

To Robert Ross

1 June 1898 [Paris]

My dear Robbie, People who repent in sackcloth are dreary, but those who repent in a suit by Doré, and intend this suit for another, are worthy of Paradise. It is most sweet of you, and the colour I would like is *blue*, like the suit I had last year.

A rather painful fact, apparent to all, must now be

12 **indignantly** (adv.): entrüstet, empört.
20 **to repent in sackcloth:** in Sack und Asche büßen.
21 **dreary:** öde.

disclosed. Pray mention it to no one but Doré, and break it to him gently. I am distinctly stouter than I was when the last suit was made. I should say a good inch and a half. I *can* still button the old Doré suit, but it is tight, and the two lower buttons drag. I would like the same stuff, if possible; it is such good stuff, and has lasted so well. TL 752

1 **to disclose s.th.:** etwas enthüllen, mitteilen, verraten.
2 **stout:** beleibt, korpulent.
5 **to drag:** hier: spannen.

III

Moving in with the Lady Killers

ALGERNON. I hope, Cecily, I shall not offend you if I state quite frankly and openly that you seem to me to be in every way the visible personification of absolute perfection.

CECILY. I think your frankness does you great credit, Ernest. If you will allow me, I will copy your remarks into my diary. *(Goes over to table and begins writing in diary.)*

ALGERNON. Do you really keep a diary? I'd give anything to look at it. May I?

CECILY. Oh, no. *(Puts her hand over it.)* You see, it is simply a very young girl's record of her own thoughts and impressions, and consequently meant for publication. When it appears in volume form I hope you will order a copy. But pray, Ernest, don't stop. I delight in taking down from dictation. I have reached "absolute perfection". You can go on. I am quite ready for more.

ALGERNON *(somewhat taken aback)*. Ahem! Ahem!

CECILY. Oh, don't cough, Ernest. When one is dictating one should speak fluently and not cough. Besides, I

7 **frankness:** Offenheit.
21 **taken aback:** verblüfft.

Oscar Wilde photographed by Napoleon Sarony, 1882

don't know how to spell a cough. *(Writes as Algernon speaks.)*

ALGERNON *(speaking very rapidly)*. Miss Cardew, ever since half-past twelve this afternoon, when I first looked upon your wonderful and incomparable beauty, I have not merely been your abject slave and servant, but, soaring upon the pinions of a possibly monstrous ambition, I have dared to love you wildly, passionately, devotedly, hopelessly.

CECILY *(laying down her pen)*. Oh! please say that all over again. You speak far too fast and far too indistinctly. Kindly say it all over again.

[…]

(*Enter Merriman.*)

MERRIMAN. The dog-cart is waiting, sir.

ALGERNON. Tell it to come round next week at the same hour.

MERRIMAN *(looks at Cecily who makes no sign)*. Yes, sir.

CECILY. Uncle Jack would be very much annoyed if he knew you were staying on till next week, at the same hour.

ALGERNON. Oh! I don't care about Jack! I don't care for anybody in the whole world but you. I love you. Cecily! you will marry me, won't you?

CECILY. You silly boy! Of course. Why, we have been engaged for the last three months.

ALGERNON. For the last three months?

5 **incomparable:** unvergleichlich.
6 **abject:** unterwürfig.
7 **to soar:** aufsteigen, sich erheben.
pinion: Flügel(spitze), Schwinge.
15 **dog-cart:** (zweirädriger) Einspänner.

CECILY. Three months all but a few days. *(Looks at diary, turns over page.)* Yes; it will be exactly three months on Thursday.

ALGERNON. I didn't know.

CECILY. Very few people nowadays ever realise the position in which they are placed. The age is, as Miss Prism often says, a thoughtless one.

ALGERNON. But how did we become engaged?

CECILY. Well, ever since dear Uncle Jack first confessed to us that he had a younger brother who was very wicked and bad, you of course have formed the chief topic of conversation between myself and Miss Prism. And of course a man who is much talked about is always very attractive. One feels there must be something in him, after all. I dare say it was foolish of me, but I fell in love with you, Ernest.

ALGERNON. Darling! And when was the engagement actually settled?

CECILY. On the 14th of February last. Worn out by your entire ignorance of my existence, I determined to end the matter one way or the other, and after a long struggle with myself I accepted you one evening in the garden. The next day I bought this little ring in your name. You see I always wear it, Ernest, and though it shows that you are sadly extravagant, still I have long ago forgiven you for that. Here in this drawer are all the little presents I have given you from time to time, neatly numbered and labelled. This is the pearl necklace you gave me on my birthday. And this is the box in which I keep all your

19 **worn out:** erschöpft, zermürbt.
28f. **labelled:** mit einem Etikett versehen.

letters. *(Opens box and produces letters tied up with blue ribbon.)*

ALGERNON. My letters! But my own sweet Cecily, I have never written you any letters.

CECILY. You need hardly remind me of that, Ernest. I remember it only too well. I grew tired of asking the postman every morning if he had a London letter for me. My health began to give way under the strain and anxiety. So I wrote your letters for you, and had them posted to me in the village by my maid. I wrote always three times a week and sometimes oftener.

ALGERNON. Oh, do let me read them, Cecily.

CECILY. Oh, I couldn't possibly. They would make you far too conceited. The three you wrote me after I had broken off the engagement are so beautiful and so badly spelt that even now I can hardly read them without crying a little.

ALGERNON. But was our engagement ever broken off?

CECILY. Of course it was. On the 22nd of last March. You can see the entry if you like. *(Shows Diary.)* "Today I broke off my engagement with Ernest. I feel it is better to do so. The weather still continues charming."

ALGERNON. But why on earth did you break it off? What had I done? I had done nothing at all. Cecily, I am very much hurt indeed to hear you broke it off. Particularly when the weather was so charming.

CECILY. Men seem to forget very easily. I should have thought you would have remembered the violent

9 **strain:** Anspannung.
15 **conceited:** eingebildet.

letter you wrote to me because I danced with Lord Kelso at the county ball.

ALGERNON. But I did take it all back, Cecily, didn't I?

CECILY. Of course you did. Otherwise I wouldn't have forgiven you or accepted this little gold bangle with the turquoise and diamond heart, that you sent me the next day. *(Shows bangle.)*

ALGERNON. Did I give you this, Cecily? It's very pretty, isn't it?

CECILY. Yes. You have wonderfully good taste, Ernest. I have always said that of you. It's the excuse I've always given for your leading such a bad life.

ALGERNON. My own one! So we have been engaged for three months, Cecily!

CECILY. Yes; how the time has flown, hasn't it?

ALGERNON. I don't think so. I have found the days very long and very dreary without you.

CECILY. You dear romantic boy ... (*puts her fingers through his hair.*) I hope your hair curls naturally. Does it?

ALGERNON. Yes darling, with a little help from others.

CECILY. I am so glad. *The Importance of Being Earnest;* CW 357–360

"My dear boy, no woman is a genius. Women are a decorative sex. They never have anything to say, but they say it charmingly. Women represent the triumph

5 **bangle:** Armreif.
6 **turquoise:** Türkis(stein).
17 **dreary:** öde.

of matter over mind, just as men represent the triumph of mind over morals."

[...] "I am analysing women at the present, so I ought to know. The subject is not so abstruse as I thought it was. I find that, ultimately, there are only two kinds of women, the plain and the coloured. The plain women are very useful. If you want to gain a reputation for respectability, you have merely to take them down to supper. The other women are very charming. They commit one mistake, however. They paint in order to try and look young. Our grandmothers painted in order to try and talk brilliantly. *Rouge* and *esprit* used to go together. That is all over now. As long as a woman can look ten years younger than her own daughter, she is perfectly satisfied. As for conversation, there are only five women in London worth talking to, and two of these can't be admitted into decent society." *The Picture of Dorian Gray*; CW 48–49

LADY CAROLINE. [...] It is much to be regretted that in our rank of life the wife should be so persistently frivolous, under the impression apparently that it is the proper thing to be. It is to that I attribute the unhappiness of so many marriages we all know of in society.

MRS. ALLONBY. Do you know, Lady Caroline, I don't think the frivolity of the wife has ever anything to do

4 **abstruse:** schwer verständlich, dunkel.
5 **ultimately** (adv.): letztendlich.
20 **persistently** (adv.): beharrlich.

with it. More marriages are ruined nowadays by the common sense of the husband than by anything else. How can a woman be expected to be happy with a man who insists on treating her as if she was a perfectly rational being?

LADY HUNSTANTON. My dear!

MRS. ALLONBY. Man, poor, awkward, reliable, necessary man belongs to a sex that has been rational for millions and millions of years. He can't help himself. It is in his race. The History of Woman is very different. We have always been picturesque protests against the mere existence of common sense. We saw its dangers from the first.

LADY STUTFIELD. Yes, the common sense of husbands is certainly most, most trying. Do tell me your conception of the Ideal Husband. I think it would be so very, very helpful.

MRS. ALLONBY. The Ideal Husband? There couldn't be such a thing. The institution is wrong.

A Woman of No Importance; CW 446

MABEL CHILTERN. Well, Tommy has proposed to me again. Tommy really does nothing but propose to me. He proposed to me last night in the music-room, when I was quite unprotected, as there was an elaborate trio going on. I didn't dare to make the small-

7 **awkward:** unbeholfen.
11 **picturesque:** malerisch.
21 **to propose to s.o.:** jdm. einen Heiratsantrag machen.
24f. **elaborate:** kunstvoll, kompliziert.

est repartee, I need hardly tell you. If I had, it would have stopped the music at once. Musical people are so absurdly unreasonable. They always want one to be perfectly dumb at the very moment when one is longing to be absolutely deaf. Then he proposed to me in broad daylight this morning, in front of that dreadful statue of Achilles. Really, the things that go on in front of that work of art are quite appalling. The police should interfere. At luncheon I saw by the glare in his eye that he was going to propose again, and I just managed to check him in time by assuring him that I was a bimetallist. Fortunately I don't know what bimetallism means. And I don't believe anybody else does either. But the observation crushed Tommy for ten minutes. He looked quite shocked. And then Tommy is so annoying in the way he proposes. If he proposed at the top of his voice, I should not mind so much. That might produce some effect on the public. But he does it in a horrid confidential way. When Tommy wants to be romantic he talks to one just like a doctor. I am very fond of Tommy, but his methods of proposing are quite out of date. I wish, Gertrude, you would speak to him, and tell him that once a week is quite often enough to propose to any one, and that it should al-

1 **repartee:** schlagfertige Antwort.
4 **dumb:** stumm, sprachlos.
9 **appalling:** entsetzlich.
10 **glare:** finsterer, starrer Blick.
12 **bimetallist:** Anhänger(in) des Bimetallismus (Währung, bei der zwei Metalle Zahlungsmittel sind).
15 **to crush:** (fig.) niederschmettern, schwer mitnehmen.
20 **confidential:** vertraulich.

ways be done in a manner that attracts some attention.

LADY CHILTERN. Dear Mabel, don't talk like that. Besides, Robert thinks very highly of Mr. Trafford. He believes he has a brilliant future before him.

MABEL CHILTERN. Oh! I wouldn't marry a man with a future before him for anything under the sun.

LADY CHILTERN. Mabel!

MABEL CHILTERN. I know, dear. You married a man with a future, didn't you! But then Robert was a genius, and you have a noble, self-sacrificing character. You can stand geniuses. I have no character at all, and Robert is the only genius I could ever bear. As a rule, I think they are quite impossible. Geniuses talk so much, don't they? Such a bad habit! And they are always thinking about themselves, when I want them to be thinking about me. *An Ideal Husband;* CW 513

To Waldo Story

22 January 1884 Royal Victoria Hotel, Sheffield

Yes! my dear Waldino, yes! Amazing of course – that was necessary.

[…]

Her name is Constance and she is quite young, very grave, and mystical, with wonderful eyes, and dark brown coils of hair: quite perfect except that she does not think Jimmy the only painter that ever really exist-

25 **coils of hair:** Haarlocken.

ed: she would like to bring Titian or somebody in by the back door: however, she knows I am the greatest poet, so in literature she is all right: and I have explained to her that you are the greatest sculptor: art instruction cannot go further.

We are, of course, desperately in love. I have been obliged to be away nearly all the time since our engagement, civilising the provinces by my remarkable lectures, but we telegraph to each other twice a day, and the telegraph clerks have become quite romantic in consequence. I hand in my messages, however, very sternly, and try to look as if "love" was a cryptogram for "buy Grand Trunks" and "darling" a cypher for "sell out at par." I am sure it succeeds. TL 155

To the Editor of the Pall Mall Gazette

[Circa 13 October 1884]

The "Girl graduate" must of course have precedence, not merely for her sex but for her sanity: her letter is extremely sensible. She makes two points: that high heels are a necessity for any lady who wishes to keep

1 **Titian:** Tiziano Vecellio (um 1487–1576), italienischer Maler der Hochrenaissance.
4 **sculptor:** Bildhauer.
12 **cryptogram:** verschlüsselter Text.
13 **cypher:** Chiffre.
14 **at par:** zum Nennwert.
17 **to have precedence:** Vorrang haben.
19 **to make a point:** ein Argument anbringen.
19f. **high heels:** hohe Absätze, hochhackige Schuhe.

her dress clean from the Stygian mud of our streets, and that without a tight corset "the ordinary number of petticoats and etceteras" cannot be properly or conveniently held up. Now it is quite true that as long as the lower garments are suspended from the hips, a corset is an absolute necessity; the mistake lies in not suspending all apparel from the shoulders. In the latter case a corset becomes useless, the body is left free and unconfined for respiration and motion, there is more health, and consequently more beauty. Indeed all the most ungainly and uncomfortable articles of dress that fashion has ever in her folly prescribed, not the tight corset merely, but the farthingale, the vertugadin, the hoop, the crinoline, and that modern monstrosity the so-called "dress-improver" also, all of them have owed their origin to the same error, the error of not seeing that it is from the shoulders, and from the shoulders only, that all garments should be hung.

And as regards high heels, I quite admit that some additional height to the shoe or boot is necessary if

1 **Stygian:** stygisch, an den Styx (Fluss in der griechischen Unterwelt) erinnernd.
5 **garment:** Kleidungsstück.
7 **apparel:** Kleidung, Gewand.
9 **respiration:** Atmung.
12 **folly:** Torheit.
to prescribe: diktieren, vorschreiben.
13 **farthingale:** Fischbeinmieder.
vertugadin: sich nach unten verbreiterndes, mit einer Wulst versehenes Kleid aus dem 17. Jh.
14 **hoop:** Reifrock.
crinoline: Krinoline, weiter Reifrock.
15 **dress-improver:** Turnüre, Gesäßpolster.
19 **as regards:** was ... anbetrifft.

long gowns are to be worn in the street; but what I object to is that the height should be given to the heel only, and not to the sole of the foot also. TL 161–162

(Salomé dances the dance of the seven veils.)

HEROD. Ah! Wonderful! Wonderful! You see that she has danced for me, your daughter. Come near, Salomé, come near, that I may give you your reward. Ah! I pay the dancers well. I will pay thee royally. I will give thee whatsoever thy soul desireth. What wouldst thou have? Speak.

SALOMÉ *(kneeling)*. I would that they presently bring me in a silver charger …

HEROD *(laughing)*. In a silver charger? Surely yes, in a silver charger. She is charming, is she not? What is it you would have in a silver charger, O sweet and fair Salomé, you who are fairer than all the daughters of Judaea? What would you have them bring thee in a silver charger? Tell me. Whatsoever it may be, they shall give it to you. My treasures belong to thee. What is it, Salomé?

SALOMÉ *(rising)*. The head of Jokanaan.

HERODIAS. Ah! that is well said, my daughter.

HEROD. No, no!

1 **gown:** Rock, Mantel.
4 **veil:** Schleier.
9 **thy** (arch.): *your.*
desireth (arch.): *desires.*
10 **wouldst thou** (arch.): *would you.*
12 **silver charger:** Silberschüssel.
21 **Jokanaan:** Johannes der Täufer.

HERODIAS. That is well said, my daughter.

HEROD. No, no, Salomé. You do not ask me that. Do not listen to your mother's voice. She is ever giving you evil counsel. Do not heed her.

SALOMÉ. I do not heed my mother. It is for mine own pleasure that I ask the head of Jokanaan in a silver charger. You have sworn, Herod. Forget not that you have sworn an oath.

HEROD. I know it. I have sworn by my gods. I know it well. But I pray you, Salomé, ask of me something else. Ask of me the half of my kingdom, and I will give it you. But ask not of me what you have asked.

SALOMÉ. I ask of you the head of Jokanaan.

HEROD. No, no, I do not wish it.

SALOMÉ. You have sworn, Herod.

HERODIAS. Yes, you have sworn. Everybody heard you. You swore it before everybody.

HEROD. Be silent! It is not to you I speak.

HERODIAS. My daughter has done well to ask the head of Jokanaan. He has covered me with insults. He has said monstrous things against me. One can see that she loves her mother well. Do not yield, my daughter. He has sworn, he has sworn.

HEROD. Be silent, speak not to me ...! Come, Salomé, be reasonable. I have never been hard to you. I have ever loved you. ... It may be that I have loved you too much. Therefore ask not this thing of me. This is

4 **counsel:** Rat.
to heed s.o.: jdm. Beachtung schenken.
8 **oath:** Eid, Schwur.
10 **to pray s.o.** (arch.): jdn. (inständig) bitten.
22 **to yield:** nachgeben, einwilligen.

a terrible thing, an awful thing to ask of me. Surely, I think you are jesting. The head of a man that is cut from his body is ill to look upon, is it not? It is not meet that the eyes of a virgin should look upon such a thing. What pleasure could you have in it? None. No, no, it is not what you desire. Hearken to me. I have an emerald, a great round emerald, which Caesar's minion sent me. If you look through this emerald you can see things which happen at a great distance. Caesar himself carries such an emerald when he goes to the circus. But my emerald is larger. I know well that it is larger. It is the largest emerald in the whole world. You would like that, would you not? Ask it of me and I will give it you.

SALOMÉ. I demand the head of Jokanaan.

HEROD. You are not listening. You are not listening. Suffer me to speak, Salomé.

SALOMÉ. The head of Jokanaan.

HEROD. No, no, you would not have that. You say that to trouble me, because I have looked at you all this evening. It is true, I have looked at you all evening. Your beauty troubled me. Your beauty has grievously troubled me, and I have looked at you too much. But I will look at you no more. Neither at things, nor at people should one look. Only in mir-

2 **to jest:** scherzen.
4 **virgin:** Jungfrau.
6 **to hearken** (arch.): zuhören.
7 **emerald:** Smaragd.
8 **Caesar:** Beiname römischer Kaiser.
minion: Mätresse.
17 **to suffer s.o. to do s.th.:** jdm. erlauben, etwas zu tun.
22 f. **grievously** (adv.): schwer, schlimm.

rors should one look, for mirrors do but show us masks. Oh! oh! bring wine! I thirst. … Salomé, Salomé, let us be friends. Come now …! Ah! what would I say? What was't? Ah! I remember …! Salomé – nay, but come nearer to me; I fear you will not hear me – Salomé, you know my white peacocks, my beautiful white peacocks, that walk in the garden between the myrtles and the tall cypress trees. […] [I]n the whole world there is no king who has peacocks like unto my peacocks. But I will give them all to you. Only you must loose me from my oath, and must not ask of me that which you have asked of me.

(He empties the cup of wine.)

SALOMÉ. Give me the head of Jokanaan.

HERODIAS. Well said, my daughter! As for you, you are ridiculous with your peacocks.

HEROD. Be silent! You cry out always; you cry out like a beast of prey. You must not. Your voice wearies me. Be silent, I say. … Salomé, think of what you are doing. This man comes perchance from God. He is a holy man. The finger of God has touched him. God has put into his mouth terrible words. In the palace as in the desert God is always with him. … At least it is possible. One does not know. It is possible that God is for him and with him. Furthermore, if he

6 **peacock:** Pfau.
8 **myrtle:** Myrte (immergrüner Strauch des Mittelmeergebiets).
11 **to loose s.o. from s.th.:** jdn. von etwas befreien, lösen, entbinden.
19 **beast of prey:** Beutetier.
to weary: ermüden.
21 **perchance** (adv.): womöglich.
26 **furthermore:** zudem, weiterhin.

died some misfortune might happen to me. In any case, he said that the day he dies a misfortune will happen to some one. That could only be to me. Remember, I slipped in blood when I entered. Also, I heard a beating of wings in the air, a beating of mighty wings. These are very evil omens, and there were others. I am sure there were others, though I did not see them. Well, Salomé, you do not wish a misfortune to happen to me? You do not wish that. Listen to me, then.

SALOMÉ. Give me the head of Jokanaan.

HEROD. Ah! you are not listening to me. Be calm. I – I am calm. I am quite calm. Listen. I have jewels hidden in this place – jewels that your mother even has never seen; jewels that are marvellous. I have a collar of pearls, set in four rows. They are like unto moons chained with rays of silver. They are like fifty moons caught in a golden net. On the ivory of her breast a queen has worn it. Thou shalt be as fair as a queen when thou wearest it. […] What desirest thou more than this, Salomé? Tell me the thing that thou desirest, and I will give it thee. All that thou askest I will give thee save one thing. I will give thee all that is mine, save one life. I will give thee the mantle of the high priest. I will give thee the veil of the sanctuary.

18 **ivory:** Elfenbein.
19 **thou shalt** (arch.): *you shall.*
20f. **what desirest thou more?** (arch.): *what more do you desire?*
22 **thee** (arch.): *you.*
24 **save:** außer.
26 **sanctuary:** (das) Allerheiligste.

THE JEWS. Oh! Oh!

SALOMÉ. Give me the head of Jokanaan.

HEROD *(sinking back in his seat)*. Let her be given what she asks! Of a truth she is her mother's child!

Salomé; CW 570–573

To Carlos Blacker

[Postmark 4 August 1897] Café Suisse, Dieppe

My dear Friend, I am simply heart-broken at what you tell me. I don't mind my life being wrecked – that is as it should be – but when I think of poor Constance I simply want to kill myself. But I suppose I must live through it all. I don't care. Nemesis has caught me in her net: to struggle is foolish. Why is it that one runs to one's ruin? Why has destruction such a fascination? Why, when one stands on a pinnacle, must one throw oneself down? No one knows, but things are so.

Of course I think it would be much better for Constance to see me, but you think not. Well, you are wiser. My life is spilt on the sand – red wine on the sand – and the sand drinks it because it is thirsty, for no other reason.

I wish I could see you. Where I shall be in September I don't know. I don't care. I fear we shall never see each other again. But all is right: the gods hold the

9 **wrecked:** zerstört.
12 **Nemesis:** (griechische Göttin der) Vergeltung.
15 **pinnacle:** Gipfel.
19 **to spill s.th.:** etwas ausschütten, vergießen.

world on their knees. I was made for destruction. My cradle was rocked by the Fates. Only in the mire can I know peace. Ever yours OSCAR

TL 628–629

LADY BRACKNELL *(sitting down)*. You can take a seat, Mr. Worthing.

(Looks in her pocket for note-book and pencil.)

JACK. Thank you, Lady Bracknell, I prefer standing.

LADY BRACKNELL *(pencil and note-book in hand)*. I feel bound to tell you that you are not down on my list of eligible young men, although I have the same list as the dear Duchess of Bolton has. We work together, in fact. However, I am quite ready to enter your name, should your answers be what a really affectionate mother requires. Do you smoke?

JACK. Well, yes, I must admit I smoke.

LADY BRACKNELL. I am glad to hear it. A man should always have an occupation of some kind. There are far too many idle men in London as it is. How old are you?

JACK. Twenty-nine.

LADY BRACKNELL. A very good age to be married at. I

2 **cradle:** Wiege.
Fates: Schicksalsgöttinnen, Moiren, Parzen.
mire: Sumpf, Schmutz.
9 f. **to feel bound to do s.th.:** sich gezwungen fühlen, etwas zu tun.
11 **eligible:** akzeptabel.
12 **Duchess:** Herzogin.
14 f. **affectionate:** liebevoll.
19 **idle:** faul, arbeitsscheu.

have always been of opinion that a man who desires to get married should know either everything or nothing. Which do you know?

JACK *(after some hesitation)*. I know nothing, Lady Bracknell.

LADY BRACKNELL. I am pleased to hear it. I do not approve of anything that tampers with natural ignorance. Ignorance is like a delicate exotic fruit; touch it and the bloom is gone. The whole theory of modern education is radically unsound. Fortunately in England, at any rate, education produces no effect whatsoever. If it did, it would prove a serious danger to the upper classes, and probably lead to acts of violence in Grosvenor Square. What is your income?

JACK. Between seven and eight thousand a year.

LADY BRACKNELL *(makes a note in her book)*. In land, or in investments?

JACK. In investments, chiefly.

LADY BRACKNELL. That is satisfactory. What between the duties expected of one during one's lifetime, and the duties exacted from one after one's death, land has ceased to be either a profit or a pleasure. It gives one position, and prevents one from keeping it up. That's all that can be said about land.

JACK. I have a country house with some land, of course,

7 **to tamper with s.th.:** an etwas herumpfuschen.
8 **delicate:** zart, empfindlich.
9 **bloom:** Frische.
10 **unsound:** zweifelhaft.
14 **Grosvenor Square:** Platz im vornehmen Londoner Stadtteil Mayfair.
22 **to exact duties:** Steuern eintreiben.

attached to it, about fifteen hundred acres, I believe; but I don't depend on that for my real income. In fact, as far as I can make out, the poachers are the only people who make anything out of it.

LADY BRACKNELL. A country house! How many bedrooms? Well, that point can be cleared up afterwards. You have a town house, I hope? A girl with a simple, unspoiled nature, like Gwendolen, could hardly be expected to reside in the country.

JACK. Well, I own a house in Belgrave Square, but it is let by the year to Lady Bloxham. Of course, I can get it back whenever I like, at six months' notice.

LADY BRACKNELL. Lady Bloxham? I don't know her.

JACK. Oh, she goes about very little. She is a lady considerably advanced in years.

LADY BRACKNELL. Ah, nowadays that is no guarantee of respectability of character. What number in Belgrave Square?

JACK. 149.

LADY BRACKNELL *(shaking her head)*. The unfashionable side. I thought there was something. However, that could easily be altered.

JACK. Do you mean the fashion, or the side?

LADY BRACKNELL *(sternly)*. Both, if necessary, I presume. What are your politics?

JACK. Well, I am afraid I really have none. I am a Liberal Unionist.

1 *(to be)* **attached to s.th.:** zu etwas gehören.
3 **poacher:** Wilddieb.
8 **unspoiled:** unverdorben.
10 **Belgrave Square:** Platz im Londoner Stadtteil Belgravia, südlich des Hyde Park gelegen.

LADY BRACKNELL. Oh, they count as Tories. They dine with us. Or come in the evening at any rate. You have, of course, no sympathy of any kind with the Radical Party?

JACK. Oh! I don't want to put the asses against the classes, if that is what you mean, Lady Bracknell.

LADY BRACKNELL. That is exactly what I do mean … ahem! … Are your parents living?

JACK. I have lost both my parents.

LADY BRACKNELL. Both? … To lose one parent may be regarded as a misfortune … to lose both seems like carelessness. Who was your father? He was evidently a man of some wealth. Was he born in what the Radical papers call the purple of commerce, or did he rise from the ranks of the aristocracy?

JACK. I am afraid I really don't know. The fact is, Lady Bracknell, I said I had lost my parents. It would be nearer the truth to say that my parents seemed to have lost me. … I don't actually know who I am by birth. I was … well, I was found.

LADY BRACKNELL. Found!

JACK. The late Mr. Thomas Cardew, an old gentleman of a very charitable and kindly disposition, found me, and gave me the name of Worthing, because he happened to have a first-class ticket for Worthing in his pocket at the time. Worthing is a place in Sussex. It is a seaside resort.

LADY BRACKNELL. Where did the charitable gentleman

1 **Tory:** Mitglied der konservativen Partei Großbritanniens.
14 **purple of commerce:** Geldadel.
23 **charitable:** wohltätig.

who had a first-class ticket for this seaside resort find you?

JACK *(gravely)*. In a hand-bag.

LADY BRACKNELL. A hand-bag?

JACK *(very seriously)*. Yes, Lady Bracknell. I was in a hand-bag – a somewhat large, black leather hand-bag, with handles to it – an ordinary hand-bag in fact.

LADY BRACKNELL. In what locality did this Mr. James, or Thomas, Cardew come across this ordinary hand-bag?

JACK. In the cloak-room at Victoria Station. It was given to him in mistake for his own.

LADY BRACKNELL. The cloak-room at Victoria Station?

JACK. Yes. The Brighton line.

LADY BRACKNELL. The line is immaterial. Mr. Worthing, I confess I feel somewhat bewildered by what you have just told me. To be born, or at any rate bred, in a hand-bag, whether it had handles or not, seems to me to display a contempt for the ordinary decencies of family life that reminds one of the worst excesses of the French Revolution. And I presume you know what that unfortunate movement led to? As for the particular locality in which the hand-bag was found, a cloak-room at a railway station might serve to conceal a social indiscretion – has probably, indeed,

12 **cloak-room:** Gepäckaufbewahrung.
16 **immaterial:** unbedeutend, nebensächlich.
17 **to feel bewildered:** verblüfft sein.
20 **to display contempt:** von Geringschätzung zeugen.
25f. **to conceal:** verbergen.
26 **social indiscretion:** Taktlosigkeit, Entgleisung.

been used for that purpose before now – but it could hardly be regarded as an assured basis for a recognised position in good society.

JACK. May I ask you then what you would advise me to do? I need hardly say I would do anything in the world to ensure Gwendolen's happiness.

LADY BRACKNELL. I would strongly advise you, Mr. Worthing, to try and acquire some relations as soon as possible, and to make a definite effort to produce at any rate one parent, of either sex, before the season is quite over. *The Importance of Being Earnest*; CW 332–334

To Robert Ross

[Circa 1 March 1899] Gland, Canton Vaud, Switzerland

My dear Robbie, Thanks for your charming letter, which I found waiting for me here on my arrival from Genoa yesterday.

[...]

I went to Genoa to see Constance's grave. It is very pretty – a marble cross with dark ivy-leaves inlaid in a good pattern. The cemetery is a garden at the foot of the lovely hills that climb into the mountains that girdle Genoa. It was very tragic seeing her name

6 **to ensure:** sicherstellen.
16 **Genoa:** Genua.
19 **marble cross:** Marmorkreuz.
ivy-leaves: Efeublätter.
22 **to girdle:** säumen.

carved on a tomb – her surname, my name, not mentioned of course – just "Constance Mary, daughter of Horace Lloyd, Q.C." and a verse from *Revelations.* I brought some flowers. I was deeply affected – with a sense, also, of the uselessness of all regrets. Nothing could have been otherwise, and Life is a very terrible thing. TL 783

MRS. CHEVELEY. I don't mind bad husbands. I have had two. They amused me immensely.

LORD GORING. You mean that you amused yourself immensely, don't you?

MRS. CHEVELEY. What do you know about my married life?

LORD GORING. Nothing; but I can read it like a book.

MRS. CHEVELEY. What book?

LORD GORING *(rising)*. The Book of Numbers.

MRS. CHEVELEY. Do you think it is quite charming of you to be so rude to a woman in your own house?

LORD GORING. In the case of very fascinating women, sex is a challenge, not a defence.

MRS. CHEVELEY. I suppose that is meant for a compliment. My dear Arthur, women are never disarmed by compliments. Men always are. That is the difference between the two sexes.

1 **to carve:** einmeißeln.
tomb: Grabmal, -stein.
3 **Q.C.:** Abk. für *Queen's Counsel:* Kronanwalt.
"Revelations" (pl.): Offenbarung (des Johannes).
22 **to disarm s.o.** (fig.): jdn. entwaffnen.

LORD GORING. Women are never disarmed by anything, as far as I know them.

MRS. CHEVELEY *(after a pause)*. Then you are going to allow your greatest friend, Robert Chiltern, to be ruined, rather than marry some one who really has considerable attractions left. I thought you would have risen to some great height of self-sacrifice, Arthur. I think you should. And the rest of your life you could spend in contemplating your own perfections.

LORD GORING. Oh! I do that as it is. And self-sacrifice is a thing that should be put down by law. It is so demoralising to the people for whom one sacrifices oneself. They always go to the bad.

MRS. CHEVELEY. As if anything could demoralise Robert Chiltern! You seem to forget that I know his real character.

LORD GORING. What you know about him is not his real character. It was an act of folly done in his youth, dishonourable, I admit, shameful, I admit, unworthy of him, I admit, and therefore … not his true character.

MRS. CHEVELEY. How you men stand up for each other!

LORD GORING. How you women war against each other!

An Ideal Husband; CW 533–534

7 **self-sacrifice:** Selbstaufopferung.

9 **to contemplate s.th.:** über etwas nachsinnen.

11 **to put down s.th.:** etwas unterdrücken.

18 **folly:** Torheit.

19 **dishonourable:** unehrenhaft.

IV

Dangerous Liaisons

GERALD. You have never been married, Lord Illingworth, have you?

LORD ILLINGWORTH. Men marry because they are tired; women because they are curious. Both are disappointed.

GERALD. But don't you think one can be happy when one is married?

LORD ILLINGWORTH. Perfectly happy. But the happiness of a married man, my dear Gerald, depends on the people he has not married.

GERALD. But if one is in love?

LORD ILLINGWORTH. One should always be in love. That is the reason one should never marry.

GERALD. Love is a very wonderful thing, isn't it?

LORD ILLINGWORTH. When one is in love one begins by deceiving oneself. And one ends by deceiving others. That is what the world calls a romance. But a really *grande passion* is comparatively rare nowadays. It is the privilege of people who have nothing to do. That is the one use of the idle classes in a country, and the only possible explanation of us Harfords.

GERALD. Harfords, Lord Illingworth?

LORD ILLINGWORTH. That is my family name. You

18 **to deceive o.s.:** sich etwas vormachen.

should study the Peerage, Gerald. It is the one book a young man about town should know thoroughly, and it is the best thing in fiction the English have ever done. And now, Gerald, you are going into a perfectly new life with me, and I want you to know how to live.

(Mrs. Arbuthnot appears on terrace behind.)

For the world has been made by fools that wise men should live in it!

(Enter L. C. Lady Hunstanton and Doctor Daubeny.)

LADY HUNSTANTON. Ah! here you are, dear Lord Illingworth. Well, I suppose you have been telling our young friend, Gerald, what his new duties are to be, and giving him a great deal of good advice over a pleasant cigarette.

LORD ILLINGWORTH. I have been giving him the best of advice, Lady Hunstanton, and the best of cigarettes.

LADY HUNSTANTON. I am so sorry I was not here to listen to you, but I suppose I am too old now to learn. Except from you, dear Archdeacon, when you are in your nice pulpit. But then I always know what you are going to say, so I don't feel alarmed. (*Sees Mrs. Arbuthnot.*) Ah! dear Mrs. Arbuthnot, do come and join us. Come, dear.

(Enter Mrs. Arbuthnot.)

Gerald has been having such a long talk with Lord Illingworth; I am sure you must feel very much flat-

1 **peerage:** Adelskalender.
10 **L.C.:** Abk. für *Left Central.*
20 **archdeacon:** Erzdiakon.
21 **pulpit:** Kanzel.
27 f. **to feel flattered:** sich geschmeichelt fühlen.

tered at the pleasant way in which everything has turned out for him. Let us sit down. *(They sit down.)* And how is your beautiful embroidery going on?

MRS. ARBUTHNOT. I am always at work, Lady Hunstanton.

LADY HUNSTANTON. Mrs. Daubeny embroiders a little, too, doesn't she?

THE ARCHDEACON. She was very deft with her needle once, quite a Dorcas. But the gout has crippled her fingers a good deal. She has not touched the tambour frame for nine or ten years. But she has many other amusements. She is very much interested in her own health.

LADY HUNSTANTON. Ah! that is always a nice distraction, is it not? Now, what are you talking about, Lord Illingworth? Do tell us.

LORD ILLINGWORTH. I was on the point of explaining to Gerald that the world has always laughed at its own tragedies, that being the only way in which it has been able to bear them. And that, consequently, whatever the world has treated seriously belongs to the comedy side of things.

LADY HUNSTANTON. Now I am quite out of my depth. I usually am when Lord Illingworth says anything.

[…]

3 **embroidery:** Stickerei.

8 **deft:** geschickt.

9 **Dorcas:** Frauengestalt aus dem Neuen Testament, die aus Nächstenliebe Kleider für Not leidende Witwen schneiderte.
gout: Gicht.

10f. **tambour frame:** Stickrahmen.

14f. **distraction:** Ablenkung, Zeitvertreib.

The last photograph before the British Crown's prosecution of Oscar Wilde in 1895, by Ellis & Walery

LADY HUNSTANTON. […] I think on the whole that the secret of life is to take things very, very easily.

MRS. ALLONBY. The secret of life is never to have an emotion that is unbecoming.

LADY STUTFIELD. The secret of life is to appreciate the pleasure of being terribly, terribly deceived.

KELVIL. The secret of life is to resist temptation, Lady Stutfield.

LORD ILLINGWORTH. There is no secret of life. Life's aim, if it has one, is simply to be always looking for temptations. There are not nearly enough. I sometimes pass a whole day without coming across a single one. It is quite dreadful. It makes one so nervous about the future.

LADY HUNSTANTON *(shakes her fan at him)*. I don't know how it is, Lord Illingworth, but everything you have said to-day seems to me excessively immoral. It has been most interesting, listening to you.

LORD ILLINGWORTH. All thought is immoral. Its very essence is destruction. If you think of anything, you kill it. Nothing survives being thought of.

LADY HUNSTANTON. I don't understand a word, Lord Illingworth. But I have no doubt it is all quite true. Personally, I have very little to reproach myself with, on the score of thinking. I don't believe in women thinking too much. Women should think in moderation, as they should do all things in moderation.

4 **unbecoming:** unpassend, ungeeignet.

24 **to reproach o.s. with s.th.:** sich etwas vorhalten, sich Vorwürfe wegen etwas machen.

25 **on the score of:** in puncto.

LORD ILLINGWORTH. Moderation is a fatal thing, Lady Hunstanton. Nothing succeeds like excess.

LADY HUNSTANTON. I hope I shall remember that. It sounds an admirable maxim. But I'm beginning to forget everything. It's a great misfortune.

LORD ILLINGWORTH. It is one of your most fascinating qualitites, Lady Hunstanton. No woman should have a memory. Memory in a woman is the beginning of dowdiness. One can always tell from a woman's bonnet whether she has got a memory or not.

LADY HUNSTANTON. How charming you are, dear Lord Illingworth. You always find out that one's most glaring fault is one's important virtue. You have the most comforting view of life.

(Enter Farquhar.)

FARQUHAR. Doctor Daubeny's carriage!

LADY HUNSTANTON. My dear Archdeacon! It is only half-past ten.

THE ARCHDEACON *(rising)*. I am afraid I must go, Lady Hunstanton. Tuesday is always one of Mrs. Daubeny's bad nights.

LADY HUNSTANTON *(rising)*. Well, I won't keep you from her. *(Goes with him towards door.)* I have told Farquhar to put a brace of partridge into the carriage. Mrs. Daubeny may fancy them.

THE ARCHDEACON. It is very kind of you, but Mrs. Daubeny never touches solids now. Lives entirely on

9 **dowdiness:** Schlampigkeit, Mangel an Eleganz.

9f. **bonnet:** Haube.

13 **glaring:** hervorstechend.

24 **a brace of partridge:** ein Paar Rebhühner.

jellies. But she is wonderfully cheerful, wonderfully cheerful. She has nothing to complain of.
(Exit with Lady Hunstanton.)

MRS. ALLONBY *(goes over to Lord Illingworth)*. There is a beautiful moon to-night.

LORD ILLINGWORTH. Let us go and look at it. To look at anything that is inconstant is charming nowadays.

A Woman of No Importance; CW 460–465

To H. C. Marillier

[? January–February 1886] Central Station Hotel, Glasgow

[…] Sometime you will find, even as I have found, that there is no such thing as a romantic experience; there are romantic memories, and there is the desire of romance – that is all. Our most fiery moments of ecstasy are merely shadows of what somewhere else we have felt, or of what we long some day to feel. So at least it seems to me. And, strangely enough, what comes of all this is a curious mixture of ardour and of indifference. I myself would sacrifice everything for a new experience, and I know there is no such thing as a new experience at all. I think I would more readily die for what I do not believe in than for what I hold to be true. I would go to the stake for a sensation and be a sceptic to the last! Only one thing remains infinitely

1 **jelly:** Gelee.
14 **fiery:** feurig, glühend.
18 **ardour:** Leidenschaftlichkeit.
indifference: Gleichgültigkeit.
23 **to go to the stake for s.th.** (fig.): das Leben für etwas riskieren.

fascinating to me, the mystery of moods. To be master of these moods is exquisite, to be mastered by them more exquisite still. Sometimes I think that the artistic life is a long and lovely suicide, and am not sorry that it is so. TL 184–185

It was the creation of such worlds as these that seemed to Dorian Gray to be the true object, or amongst the true objects, of life; and in his search for sensations that would be at once new and delightful, and possess that element of strangeness that is so essential to romance, he would often adopt certain modes of thought that he knew to be really alien to his nature, abandon himself to their subtle influences, and then, having, as it were, caught their colour and satisfied his intellectual curiosity, leave them with that curious indifference that is not incompatible with a real ardour of temperament, and that indeed, according to certain modern psychologists, is often a condition of it.

It was rumoured of him once that he was about to join the Roman Catholic communion; and certainly the Roman ritual had always a great attraction for him. The daily sacrifice, more awful really than all the sacrifices of the antique world, stirred him as much by its

12 **alien:** fremd.
12f. **to abandon o.s. to s.th.:** sich etwas überlassen.
13 **subtle:** subtil, fein, geheimnisvoll.
16 **incompatible:** unvereinbar.
ardour: Leidenschaftlichkeit.
23 **to stir:** anrühren.

superb rejection of the evidence of the senses as by the primitive simplicity of its elements and the eternal pathos of the human tragedy that it sought to symbolise. He loved to kneel down on the cold marble pavement, and watch the priest, in his stiff flowered vestment, slowly and with white hands moving aside the veil of the tabernacle, or raising aloft the jewelled lantern-shaped monstrance with that pallid wafer that at times, one would fain think, is indeed the "*panis celestis*," the bread of angels, or, robed in the garments of the Passion of Christ, breaking the Host into the chalice, and smiting his breast for his sins. The fuming censers, that the grave boys, in their lace and scarlet, tossed into the air like great gilt flowers, had their subtle fascination for him. As he passed out, he used to look with wonder at the black confessionals, and long to sit in the dim shadow of one of them and listen to men and women whispering through the worn grating the true story of their lives.

1 **superb:** stattlich, stolz.
5 **vestment:** Messgewand.
6 **veil:** Schleier, Tuch, Vorhang.
7 **aloft:** empor.
8 **pallid:** fahl, weißlich.
wafer: Oblate, Hostie.
10 **garment:** Gewand.
11 **chalice:** Kelch.
12 **to smite one's breast:** sich die Brust schlagen.
censer: Weihrauchfass.
13 **lace:** (Stoff-)Spitze.
scarlet: Scharlachrot.
to toss: werfen, schwingen.
14 **gilt:** golden.
16 **confessional:** Beichtstuhl.
18 **grating:** Gitter.

But he never fell into the error of arresting his intellectual development by any formal acceptance of creed or system, or of mistaking, for a house in which to live, an inn that is but suitable for the sojourn of a night, or for a few hours of a night in which there are no stars and the moon is in travail.

The Picture of Dorian Gray; CW 105–106

If one puts forward an idea to a true Englishman – always a rash thing to do – he never dreams of considering whether the idea is right or wrong. The only thing he considers of any importance is whether one believes it oneself. Now, the value of an idea has nothing whatsoever to do with the sincerity of the man who expresses it. Indeed, the probabilities are that the more insincere the man is, the more purely intellectual will the idea be, as in that case it will not be coloured by either his wants, his desires, or his prejudices. However, I don't propose to discuss politics, sociology, or metaphysics with you. I like persons better than principles, and I like persons with no principles better than anything else in the world. *The Picture of Dorian Gray*; CW 23

2 **creed:** Glaube, Bekenntnis.
4 **sojourn:** Aufenthalt.
6 **to be in travail:** in Geburtswehen liegen, in den Wehen sein.
9 **rash:** übereilt, kühn.
13 **sincerity:** Aufrichtigkeit, Ernst.

"What we have to do, what at any rate it is our duty to do, is to revive this old art of Lying. Much, of course, may be done in the way of educating the public, by amateurs in the domestic circle, at literary lunches, and at afternoon teas. But this is merely the light and graceful side of lying, such as was probably heard at Cretan dinner-parties. There are many other forms. Lying for the sake of gaining some immediate personal advantage, for instance – lying with a moral purpose, as it is usually called – though of late it has been rather looked down upon, was extremely popular with the antique world. Athena laughs when Odysseus tells her 'his words of sly devising', as Mr. William Morris phrases it, and the glory of mendacity illumines the pale brow of the stainless hero of Euripidean tragedy, and sets among the noble women of the past the young bride of one of Horace's most exquisite odes. Later on, what at first had been merely a natural instinct was elevated into a self-conscious science. Elaborate rules were laid down for the guidance of mankind, and an important school of literature grew up round the subject. Indeed, when one remembers the excellent philo-

7 **Cretan:** kretisch (Anspielung auf das berühmte Paradox »Ein Kreter sagt: ›Alle Kreter sind Lügner‹«).

13 **sly:** gerissen, schlau.
Morris: William M. (1834–1896), englischer Literat, Maler und Sozialist; Mitbegründer der englischen Kunstgewerbebewegung (*Arts and Crafts Movement*).

14 **mendacity:** Verlogenheit.

15 **Euripidean:** Adjektiv zu Euripides (484–406), neben Sophokles und Aischylos bedeutendster Tragödiendichter der griechischen Klassik.

17 **Horace:** Quintus Horatio Flaccus (65–8), römischer Lyriker (Oden, Epoden und Satiren); Freund des Gaius Maecenas.

19 **to elevate s.th.:** etwas erheben.

sophical treatise of Sanchez on the whole question, one cannot help regretting that no one has ever thought of publishing a cheap and condensed edition of the works of that great casuist. A short primer, 'When to Lie and How,' if brought out in an attractive and not too expensive a form, would no doubt command a large sale, and would prove of real practical service to many earnest and deep-thinking people. Lying for the sake of the improvement of the young, which is the basis of home education, still lingers amongst us, and its advantages are so admirably set forth in the early books of Plato's *Republic* that it is unnecessary to dwell upon them here. It is a mode of lying for which all good mothers have peculiar capabilities, but it is capable of still further development, and has been sadly overlooked by the School Board. Lying for the sake of a monthly salary is, of course, well known in Fleet Street, and the profession of a political leader-writer is not without its advantages. But it is said to be a somewhat dull occupation, and it certainly does not lead to much beyond a kind of ostentatious obscurity. The only form of lying that is absolutely be-

1 **treatise:** Traktat, Abhandlung.
Sanchez: Francisco Sanches (um 1550–1623), portugiesischer Arzt und Philosoph; Vertreter des konstruktiven Skeptizismus (Hauptwerk: *Quod Nihil Scitur*, 1589).
4 **casuist:** spitzfindiger Gelehrter.
primer: Fibel, Leitfaden.
13 **to dwell upon s.th.:** (fig.) bei etwas verweilen.
16 **School Board:** Schulamt, -aufsichtsbehörde.
18 **Fleet Street:** Hauptverkehrsstraße im Zentrum Londons, in der die meisten überregionalen Zeitungsverlage ansässig sind.
21 **ostentatious:** prahlerisch.
22 **obscurity:** Obskurität, Unbekanntheit, zweifelhafter Status.

yond reproach is lying for its own sake, and the highest development of this is, as we have already pointed out, Lying in Art. Just as those who do not love Plato more than Truth cannot pass beyond the threshold of the Academe, so those who do not love Beauty more than Truth never know the inmost shrine of Art. The solid, stolid British intellect lies in the desert sands like the Sphinx in Flaubert's marvellous tale, and fantasy, *La Chimère*, dances round it, and calls to it with her false, flute-toned voice. It may not hear her now, but surely some day, when we are all bored to death with the commonplace character of modern fiction, it will hearken to her and try to borrow her wings.

And when that day dawns, or sunset reddens, how joyous we shall all be! Facts will be regarded as discreditable, Truth will be found mourning over her fetters, and Romance, with her temper of wonder, will return to the land. The very aspect of the world will change to our startled eyes. Out of the sea will rise Behemoth and Leviathan, and sail round the high-pooped galleys, as they do on the delightful maps of those ages when books on geography were actually

4 **threshold:** (Tür-)Schwelle.
5 **Academe** (arch.): (Platonische) Akademie.
7 **stolid:** phlegmatisch, unerschütterlich.
8 **Flaubert:** Gustave F. (1821–80), französischer Romancier.
13 **to hearken** (arch.): zuhören.
15f. **discreditable:** schändlich, schimpflich.
16 **to mourn:** trauern.
17 **fetter:** (Fuß-)Fessel.
19 **startled:** erstaunt.
20 **Behemoth and Leviathan:** biblische Ungeheuer.
20f. **high-pooped galleys:** Galeeren mit hohem Heckaufbau.

readable. Dragons will wander about the waste places, and the phoenix will soar from her nest of fire into the air. We shall lay our hands upon the basilisk, and see the jewel in the toad's head. Champing his gilded oats, the Hippogriff will stand in our stalls, and over our heads will float the Blue Bird singing of beautiful and impossible things, of things that are lovely and that never happen, of things that are not and that should be. But before this comes to pass we must cultivate the lost art of Lying." *The Decay of Lying*; CW 990–991

1 **dragon:** Drache.
2 **to soar:** aufsteigen.
3 **basilisk:** Fabeltier mit tödlichem Blick.
4 **toad:** Kröte.
to champ: (zer)kauen.
gilded: golden.
oats (pl.): Hafer.
5 **Hippogriff:** Pegasusähnliches Fabelwesen aus Ludovico Ariosts *Orlando Furioso* (1516).
6 **blue bird:** Singvogel aus der Familie der Grasmücken.

V

Mother Nature and Her Rivals

To More Adey

[March 1899] Gland, Switzerland

My dear More, I am so glad you liked the play, and that it arrived safe. As a rule Smithers suppresses all my presentation copies. I am staying, as I dare say you know, in a villa on the Lake of Geneva. There is much beauty of an obvious, old-fashioned kind – snow-capped mountains, blue sky, pine-trees and the like. But the sunlight is golden: brazen rather. I don't like my host, and the Swiss are so ugly to look at that it conveys melancholy into all my days.

[…]

I was very happy on the Riviera – lovely weather – and at Nice beautiful people and beautiful flowers. As one nears Italy physical beauty comes running to meet one. At Nice I knew three lads like bronzes, quite perfect in form. English lads are chryselephantine.

6 **as a rule:** üblicherweise.
to suppress: unterschlagen.
11 **brazen:** messingfarben.
16 **Nice:** Nizza.
18 **bronze:** Bronzestatue.
19 **chryselephantine:** mit Gold und Elfenbein verziert.

Oscar Wilde photographed by Napoleon Sarony, 1882

Swiss people are carved out of wood with a rough knife, most of them; the others are carved out of turnips.

TL 784

For the wonderful beauty that had so fascinated Basil Hallward, and many others besides him, seemed never to leave him. Even those who had heard the most evil things against him, and from time to time strange rumours about his mode of life crept through London and became the chatter of the clubs, could not believe anything to his dishonour when they saw him. He had always the look of one who had kept himself unspotted from the world. Men who talked grossly became silent when Dorian Gray entered the room. There was something in the purity of his face that rebuked them. His mere presence seemed to recall to them the memory of the innocence that they had tarnished. They wondered how one so charming and graceful as he was could have escaped the stain of an age that was at once sordid and sensual.

Often, on returning home from one of those mysterious and prolonged absences that gave rise to such

1 **to carve:** schnitzen.
2f. **turnip:** Steckrübe.
9 **chatter:** Klatsch, Gerede.
12 **to talk grossly:** hinter dem Rücken reden, anzügliche Bemerkungen machen.
14 **purity:** Reinheit.
14f. **to rebuke:** zurechtweisen.
16f. **to tarnish:** beflecken.
19 **sordid:** garstig, scheußlich.

strange conjecture among those who were his friends, or thought that they were so, he himself would creep upstairs to the locked room, open the door with the key that never left him now, and stand, with a mirror, in front of the portrait that Basil Hallward had painted of him, looking now at the evil and ageing face on the canvas, and now at the fair young face that laughed back at him from the polished glass. The very sharpness of the contrast used to quicken his sense of pleasure. He grew more and more enamoured of his own beauty, more and more interested in the corruption of his own soul. He would examine with minute care, and sometimes with a monstrous and terrible delight, the hideous lines that seared the wrinkling forehead, or crawled around the heavy sensual mouth, wondering sometimes which were the more horrible, the signs of sin or the signs of age. He would place his white hands beside the coarse bloated hands of the picture, and smile. He mocked the misshapen body and the failing limbs. *The Picture of Dorian Gray*; CW 102–103

1 **conjecture:** Mutmaßung.
7 **canvas:** Leinwand.
9 **to quicken:** beleben, wecken.
10 **to grow enamoured of s.th.:** sich in etwas verlieben.
12 **with minute care:** mit peinlicher Sorgfalt.
14 **hideous:** abscheulich.
to sear: verdorren, verwelken lassen.
to wrinkle: runzelig werden.
18 **bloated:** aufgedunsen.
19 **to mock:** verspotten, -höhnen.
misshapen: missgestaltet, unförmig.

To Reginald Turner

[Postmark 19 January 1899] Hôtel des Bains, Napoule

My dear Reggie, I was charmed to hear from you, but it is absurd your being in bad spirits about Life. You used to be such a light-hearted lad. The influence of the *D. T.* is obviously of the worst kind.

I am still sitting on porphyry rocks, or roaming through pine-woods. Occasionally my friend Harold Mellor orders a bottle of Pommery for dinner. Then the exquisite taste of ancient life comes back to me. And twice a week I look at the shop-windows in Cannes.

The weather is lovely, and the mimosa in flower – such powdered gold-dust dancing in the sun, the dainty feather-like leaves always tremulous with joy.

I am very anxious to go to Corsica. Would you like a long Corsican knife marked "*Vendetta*"? They are deadly and inexpensive, and you have many friends. It might be useful.

If you hear any news of poor Sir John do let me know. Ever yours

OSCAR

TL 776–777

2 **Napoule:** Seebad an der Côte d'Azur.
4 **to be in bad spirits:** gedrückter Stimmung sein.
6 **D.T.:** Abk. für *delirium tremens*.
7 **porphyry:** porphyrisch, aus Porphyr (Ergussgestein mit Kristalleinsprengseln) bestehend.
to roam: umherstreifen.
9 **Pommery:** französische Champagnermarke.
13 **mimosa:** Mimose.
14 **dainty:** zierlich.
15 (*to be*) **tremulous with joy:** vor Freude zittern.
17 **vendetta:** Blutfehde.

He felt strangely calm, and, walking over to the window, opened it, and stepped out on the balcony. The wind had blown the fog away, and the sky was like a monstrous peacock's tail, starred with myriads of golden eyes. He looked down, and saw the policeman going his rounds and flashing the long beam of his lantern on the doors of the silent houses. The crimson spot of a prowling hansom gleamed at the corner, and then vanished. A woman in a fluttering shawl was creeping slowly by the railings, staggering as she went. Now and then she stopped, and peered back. Once, she began to sing in a hoarse voice. The policeman strolled over and said something to her. She stumbled away, laughing. A bitter blast swept across the Square. The gas-lamps flickered, and became blue, and the leafless trees shook their black iron branches to and fro. He shivered, and went back, closing the window behind him.

Having reached the door, he turned the key, and opened it. He did not even glance at the murdered man. He felt that the secret of the whole thing was not

4 **peacock:** Pfau.
myriad: Unzahl, große Menge.
7 **crimson:** purpurrot.
8 **to prowl:** (ziellos) umherfahren.
hansom: Droschke.
to gleam: leuchten, schimmern.
9 **shawl:** Schulter-, Umhangtuch.
10 **to stagger:** torkeln, schwanken.
11 **to peer:** spähen, lugen.
12 **hoarse:** heiser.
13 **to stroll:** schlendern.
16f. **to and fro:** hin und her.

to realise the situation. The friend who had painted the fatal portrait to which all his misery had been due had gone out of his life. That was enough.

The Picture of Dorian Gray; CW 123

To H.C. Pollitt

[Postmark of receipt 31 December 1898]

Hôtel des Bains, Napoule

Dear Mr Pollitt, I have come down to the Riviera, with your photograph, of course (the nice one in the Norfolk suit), and the day is blue and gold, the sun warm like wine, and apricot-coloured: the pine-woods change the air to an aromatic: the wind that stirs their branches is pungent with keen odours: and when one walks in green aisles one crushes sweetness out of the fallen needles. Of course, *you* should be here also. I search for you daily.

It is a little fishing village, on the Golfe de Juan, close to Cannes. The inhabitants have beautiful eyes, crisp hair of a hyacinth colour, and no morals – an ideal race. At times, being morbid, I am bored by the lack of intellect: but that is a grave fault: I attribute it to Oxford. None of us survive culture.

2 **to be due to s.th.:** sich auf etwas zurückführen lassen.
11 **apricot-coloured:** aprikosenfarben.
13 **pungent:** stechend, prickelnd.
odour: Geruch, Duft.
14 **aisle:** Schneise, Weg zwischen Bäumen.
19 **crisp:** kraus, lockig.
20 **morbid:** morbid, angekränkelt.

What are you doing in the Green Window? Are you writing? Or simply looking at Nature? I am on bad terms with Nature: I see in her neither intellect nor passion – the only two things that make surfaces possible for me. I allude of course to what is termed Landscape.

Send *me* a nice letter and a nice book. Sincerely yours OSCAR WILDE

TL 774

A cold rain began to fall, and the blurred street-lamps looked ghastly in the dipping mist. The public-houses were just closing and dim men and women were clustering in broken groups round their doors. From some of the bars came the sound of horrible laughter. In others, drunkards brawled and screamed.

Lying back in the hansom, with his hat pulled over his forehead, Dorian Gray watched with listless eyes the sordid shame of the great city, and now and then he repeated to himself the words that Lord Henry had

1 **Green Window:** Name von Pollitts Haus in Kendal.
5 **to allude to s.th.:** auf etwas anspielen.
10 **blurred:** schemenhaft, verschwommen.
11 **ghastly:** gespenstisch.
dipping: sinkend; triefend.
public-house: Gaststätte.
12f. **to cluster:** sich drängen, scharen.
15 **drunkard:** Trinker(in).
to brawl: lärmen, zanken.
16 **hansom:** Droschke.
17 **listless:** teilnahmslos.
18 **sordid:** schmutzig, elend.

said to him on the first day they had met, "To cure the soul by means of the senses, and the senses by means of the soul." Yes, that was the secret. He had often tried it, and would try it again now. There were opium-dens, where one could buy oblivion, dens of horror where the memory of old sins could be destroyed by the madness of sins that were new.

The moon hung low in the sky like a yellow skull. From time to time a huge misshapen cloud stretched a long arm across and hid it. The gas-lamps grew fewer, and the streets more narrow and gloomy. Once the man lost his way, and had to drive back half a mile. A steam rose from the horse as it splashed up the puddles. The side-windows of the hansom were clogged with a grey-flannel mist.

"To cure the soul by means of the senses, and the senses by means of the soul!" How the words rang in his ears! His soul, certainly, was sick to death. Was it true that the senses could cure it? Innocent blood had been spilt. What could atone for that? Ah! for that there was no atonement; but though forgiveness was

4f. **opium-den:** Opiumhöhle.
5 **oblivion:** Vergessen.
8 **skull:** Schädel.
9 **misshapen:** unförmig.
10 **gas-lamp:** Gaslaterne.
11 **gloomy:** düster.
13 **to splash up:** hoch aufspritzen lassen.
13f. **puddle:** Pfütze.
14 **clogged:** verschmiert, verkleistert.
15 **grey-flannel:** flanellgrau.
20 **to spill s.th.:** etwas vergießen.
to atone for s.th.: etwas wieder gutmachen, aufwiegen.

impossible, forgetfulness was possible still, and he was determined to forget, to stamp the thing out, to crush it as one would crush the adder that had stung one. Indeed, what right had Basil to have spoken to him as he had done? Who had made him a judge over others? He had said things that were dreadful, horrible, not to be endured.

On and on plodded the hansom, going slower, it seemed to him, at each step. He thrust up the trap, and called to the man to drive faster. The hideous hunger for opium began to gnaw at him. His throat burned, and his delicate hands twitched nervously together. He struck at the horse madly with his stick. The driver laughed, and whipped up. He laughed in answer, and the man was silent.

The way seemed interminable, and the streets like the black web of some sprawling spider. The monotony became unbearable, and, as the mist thickened, he felt afraid.

Then they passed by lonely brickfields. The fog was lighter here, and he could see the strange bottle-

3 **adder:** Natter, Viper.
8 **to plod:** (schwerfällig) rollen.
9 **to thrust up:** aufstoßen, hochschlagen.
trap: Klappe.
10 **hideous:** scheußlich, abscheulich.
11 **to gnaw at s.o.:** an jdm. nagen.
12 **to twitch:** zucken.
16 **interminable:** endlos.
17 **web:** (Spinnen-)Netz.
to sprawl: ausgestreckt liegen.
18 **unbearable:** unerträglich.
to thicken: dichter werden.
20 **brickfield:** Ziegelei.

shaped kilns with their orange fan-like tongues of fire. A dog barked as they went by, and far away in the darkness some wandering sea-gull screamed. The horse stumbled in a rut, then swerved aside, and broke into a gallop.

After some time they left the clay road, and rattled again over rough-paven streets. Most of the windows were dark, but now and then fantastic shadows were silhouetted against some lamp-lit blind. He watched them curiously. They moved like monstrous marionettes, and made gestures like live things. He hated them. A dull rage was in his heart. As they turned a corner a woman yelled something at them from an open door, and two men ran after the hansom for about a hundred yards. The driver beat at them with his whip.

It is said that passion makes one think in a circle. Certainly with hideous iteration the bitten lips of Dorian Gray shaped and reshaped those subtle words that dealt with soul and sense, till he had found in them the full expression, as it were, of his mood, and justified,

1 **kiln:** Brennofen.
3 **sea-gull:** Seemöwe.
4 **rut:** Wagenspur.
to swerve: seitlich ausbrechen.
4f. **to break into a gallop:** in Galopp fallen.
6 **clay:** Lehm.
to rattle: rattern.
7 **rough-paven:** grob gepflastert.
8f. **to be silhouetted against s.th.:** sich (als Silhouette) gegen, vor etwas abzeichnen.
9 **blind:** Vorhang, Rouleau.
18 **iteration:** Wiederholung.
19 **subtle:** geheimnisvoll.

by intellectual approval, passions that without such justification would still have dominated his temper. From cell to cell of his brain crept the one thought; and the wild desire to live, most terrible of all man's appetites, quickened into force each trembling nerve and fibre. Ugliness that had once been hateful to him because it made things real, became dear to him now for that very reason. Ugliness was the one reality. The coarse brawl, the loathsome den, the crude violence of disordered life, the very vileness of thief and outcast, were more vivid, in their intense actuality of impression, than all the gracious shapes of Art, the dreamy shadows of Song. They were what he needed for forgetfulness. In three days he would be free.

Suddenly the man drew up with a jerk at the top of a dark lane. Over the low roofs and jagged chimney stacks of the houses rose the black masts of ships. Wreaths of white mist clung like ghostly sails to the yards. *The Picture of Dorian Gray*; CW 140–142

5 **to quicken:** beleben, erwecken.
9 **brawl:** Geschrei, Gezänk.
loathsome: widerwärtig.
crude: roh, ordinär.
10 **vileness:** Niedertracht, Verworfenheit.
outcast: Ausgestoßene(r).
11 **vivid:** lebhaft, lebendig.
12 **gracious:** liebenswürdig, kultiviert.
15 **jerk:** Ruck.
16f. **jagged chimney stacks:** gezackte Schornsteinreihen.
18 **wreath:** Kranz, Girlande.
19 **yard:** Rahe (waagerechte Stange am Mast).

CYRIL. Nature follows the landscape painter, then, and takes her effects from him?

VIVIAN. Certainly. Where, if not from the Impressionists, do we get those wonderful brown fogs that come creeping down our streets, blurring the gas-lamps and changing the houses into monstrous shadows? To whom, if not to them and their master, do we owe the lovely silver mists that brood over our river, and turn to faint forms of fading grace curved bridge and swaying barge? The extraordinary change that has taken place in the climate of London during the last ten years is entirely due to a particular school of Art. You smile. Consider the matter from a scientific or a metaphysical point of view, and you will find that I am right. For what is Nature? Nature is no great mother who has borne us. She is our creation. It is in our brain that she quickens to life. Things are because we see them, and what we see, and how we see it, depends on the Arts that have influenced us. To look at a thing is very different from seeing a thing. One does not see anything until one sees its beauty. Then, and then only, does it come into existence. At present, people see fogs, not be-

3f. **Impressionist:** Vertreter des Impressionismus, einer 1860–70 in der französischen Malerei entstandenen Stilrichtung (Freiluftmalerei).
5 **to blur:** verschleiern, undeutlich werden lassen.
5f. **gas-lamp:** Gaslaterne.
8 **to brood:** schweben, brüten.
9 **fading grace:** verblassende Anmut.
10 **to sway:** schwanken, sich wiegen.
barge: Barke, Lastkahn.
12 **to be due to s.th.:** auf etwas zurückzuführen sein.
17 **to quicken to life:** zum Leben erwachen.

cause there are fogs, but because poets and painters have taught them the mysterious loveliness of such effects. There may have been fogs for centuries in London. I dare say there were. But no one saw them, and so we do not know anything about them. They did not exist till Art had invented them. Now, it must be admitted, fogs are carried to excess. They have become the mere mannerism of a clique, and the exaggerated realism of their method gives dull people bronchitis. Where the cultured catch an effect, the uncultured catch cold. And so, let us be humane, and invite Art to turn her wonderful eyes elsewhere. She has done so already, indeed. That white quivering sunlight that one sees now in France, with its strange blotches of mauve, and its restless violet shadows, is her latest fancy, and, on the whole, Nature reproduces it quite admirably. Where she used to give us Corots and Daubignys, she gives us now exquisite Monets and entrancing Pissaros. Indeed there are moments, rare, it is true, but still to be observed from time to time, when Nature becomes absolutely modern. Of course she is

8 **mannerism:** Manieriertheit, Unnatürlichkeit.
clique: Clique, Klüngel.

14 **to quiver:** zittern.

15 **blotch:** Fleck.
mauve: mauve, malvenfarbig.

18/19 **Corot / Daubigny / Monet:** Camille C. (1796–1875), Charles François D. (1817–78), Claude M. (1840–1926), französische Impressionisten.

19 **entrancing:** entzückend, bezaubernd.

20 **Pissaro:** *Pissarro:* Camille P. (1830–1903), französischer Impressionist.

not always to be relied upon. The fact is that she is in this unfortunate position. Art creates an incomparable and unique effect, and, having done so, passes on to other things. Nature, upon the other hand, forgetting that imitation can be made the sincerest form of insult, keeps on repeating this effect until we all become absolutely wearied of it. Nobody of any real culture, for instance, ever talks nowadays about the beauty of a sunset. Sunsets are quite old-fashioned. They belong to the time when Turner was the last note in art. To admire them is a distinct sign of provincialism of temperament.

The Decay of Lying; CW 986

And so he would now study perfumes, and the secrets of their manufacture, distilling heavily-scented oils, and burning odorous gums from the East. He saw that there was no mood of the mind that had not its counterpart in the sensuous life, and set himself to discover their true relation, wondering what there was in

2f. **incomparable:** unvergleichlich.
3 **unique:** einzigartig.
10 **Turner:** William T. (1775–1851), englischer Maler.
11 **the last note:** der letzte Schrei.
12 **provincialism:** spießige Einstellung.
15 **to distil:** destillieren.
heavily-scented: stark duftend.
16 **odorous:** duftend, wohlriechend.
gum: Gummiharz.
18 **counterpart:** Gegenstück.
sensuous: sinnlich, sinnenfreudig.

frankincense that made one mystical, and in ambergris that stirred one's passions, and in violets that woke the memory of dead romances, and in musk that troubled the brain, and in champak that stained the imagination; and seeking often to elaborate a real psychology of perfumes, and to estimate the several influences of sweet-smelling roots, and scented pollen-laden flowers, or aromatic balms, and of dark and fragrant woods, of spikenard that sickens, of hovenia that makes men mad, and of aloes that are said to be able to expel melancholy from the soul.

At another time he devoted himself entirely to music, and in a long latticed room, with a vermilion-and-gold ceiling and walls of olive-green lacquer, he used to give curious concerts, in which mad gypsies tore wild music from little zithers, or grave yellow-shawled Tunisians plucked at the strained strings of monstrous lutes, while grinning negroes beat monotonously upon

1 **frankincense:** Weihrauch.
ambergris: Ambra.
3 **musk:** Moschus.
4 **champak:** Champacaöl (ätherisches Öl).
8 **balm:** Balsam, Salbe.
fragrant: duftend, wohlriechend.
9 **spikenard:** Narde, Großer Speik.
hovenia: Hovenia (asiatisches Kreuzdorngewächs).
10 **aloe:** Aloe (tropisches Liliengewächs).
to expel: vertreiben.
13 **latticed:** vergittert.
13f. **vermilion-and-gold:** zinnoberrot und golden.
14 **lacquer:** Lack.
15 **gipsy:** Zigeuner(in).
16 **yellow-shawled:** mit gelbem Schal.
17 **strained strings:** straffe Saiten.
18 **lute:** Laute.

copper drums, and, crouching upon scarlet mats, slim turbaned Indians blew through long pipes of reed or brass, and charmed, or feigned to charm, great hooded snakes and horrible horned adders. The harsh intervals and shrill discords of barbaric music stirred him at times when Schubert's grace, and Chopin's beautiful sorrows, and the mighty harmonies of Beethoven himself, fell unheeded on his ear. […]

On one occasion he took up the study of jewels, and appeared at a costume ball as Anne de Joyeuse, Admiral of France, in a dress covered with five hundred and sixty pearls. This taste enthralled him for years, and, indeed, may be said never to have left him. He would often spend a whole day settling and resettling in their cases the various stones that he had collected, such as the olive-green chrysoberyl that turns red by lamplight, the cymophane with its wire-like line of silver, the pistachio-coloured peridot, rose-pink and

1 **to crouch:** kauern.
scarlet: scharlachrot.
2 **reed:** Schilfrohr.
3 **to feign:** vortäuschen.
3f. **hooded snake:** Kobra.
4 **adder:** Natter, Viper.
harsh intervals: unreine Intervalle.
5 **discords:** Missklänge.
8 **unheeded:** unbeachtet.
10 **Anne de Joyeuse:** französischer Herzog; Favorit des homosexuellen Königs Henri III.
12 **to enthrall:** bezaubern, fesseln.
14 **to settle:** ordnen.
16 **chrysoberyl:** Chrysoberyll (grüner Edelstein).
17 **cymophane:** Katzenauge (Mineral).
18 **pistachio-coloured:** pistazienfarben, -grün.
peridot: Peridot (Mineral).

wine-yellow topazes, carbuncles of fiery scarlet with tremulous four-rayed stars, flame-red cinnamon-stones, orange and violet spinels, and amethysts with their alternate layers of ruby and sapphire. He loved the red gold of the sunstone, and the moonstone's pearly whiteness, and the broken rainbow of the milky opal. He procured from Amsterdam three emeralds of extraordinary size and richness of colour, and had a turquoise *de la vieille roche* that was the envy of all the connoisseurs. *The Picture of Dorian Gray*; CW 106–107

VIVIAN. Enjoy Nature! I am glad to say that I have entirely lost that faculty. People tell us that Art makes us love Nature more than we loved her before; that it reveals her secrets to us; and that after a careful

1 **topaz:** Topas (Mineral; Edelstein).
carbuncle: Karfunkelstein.
fiery: feurig, glühend.
scarlet: Scharlachrot.
2 **tremulous:** zitternd.
cinnamon-stone: (rotbrauner) Granat (Edelstein).
3 **spinel:** Spinell (Mineral).
amethyst: Amethyst (Halbedelstein).
3f. **alternate:** wechselnd.
4 **ruby:** Rubin(rot).
sapphire: Saphir(blau).
5 **sunstone:** Sonnenstein, Aventurinfeldspat.
moonstone: Mondstein (Feldspatvarietät).
7 **to procure:** erwerben, beschaffen.
emerald: Smaragd.
9 **turquoise:** Türkis.
de la vieille roche (Fr.): von feinster Qualität.
10 **connoisseur:** Kenner, Experte.

study of Corot and Constable we see things in her that had escaped our observation. My own experience is that the more we study Art, the less we care for Nature. What Art really reveals to us is Nature's lack of design, her curious crudities, her extraordinary monotony, her absolutely unfinished condition. Nature has good intentions, of course, but, as Aristotle once said, she cannot carry them out. When I look at a landscape I cannot help seeing all its defects. It is fortunate for us, however, that Nature is so imperfect, as otherwise we should have no art at all. Art is our spirited protest, our gallant attempt to teach Nature her proper place. As for the infinite variety of Nature, that is a pure myth. It is not to be found in Nature herself. It resides in the imagination, or fancy, or cultivated blindness of the man who looks at her. *The Decay of Lying;* CW 970

Tuesday morning [1 June 1897]. 9.30.

The sea and sky one opal, no horrid drawing-master's line between them, just one fishing boat, going slowly, and drawing the wind after it. I am going to bathe.

TL 548

1 **Corot:** Camille C. (1796–1875), französischer Impressionist.
Constable: John C. (1776–1837), englischer Maler.
5 **crudity:** Rohheit, Unfertigkeit.
12 **spirited:** beherzt, mutig.
gallant: tapfer.
14 **myth:** Mythos, Gerücht.
19 **drawing-master:** Zeichenlehrer.

VI

Campaigning against the Philistines

To Mrs George Lewis

12 February 1882 Grand Pacific Hotel, Chicago

My dear Mrs Lewis, I sent you a letter this morning, but must write you a little line to tell you how delighted I was to get *your* letter. It touched me and pleased me more than I can tell you to receive such kindly words, I being so far away. It seemed a little touch and breath of home, and came with the sweet memory of people for whom I have the warmest affection, and most loving respect.

The English papers are too ridiculous. You know the Americans – they don't spend their money without a return. For lecturing in Chicago I received before I stepped on the platform a fee of 1000 dollars – £ 200: for one hour's work – that is answer enough. Of course in smaller places I get less, but never less than £ 40. Here I get £ 200, as at Boston. I could lecture from now till day of doom if I had strength and time to do it, and though the east has been horrid in the newspapers, the west is

14f. **they don't spend their money without a return:** sie wollen etwas sehen für ihr Geld.
19f. **day of doom:** *doomsday:* Jüngster Tag.
21 **horrid:** entsetzlich, fürchterlich.

very good and simple. I have a sort of triumphal progress, live like a young sybarite, travel like a young god. At Boston I had an immense success: here I expect one. I am deluged with poems and flowers at every town, have a secretary writing autographs all day, and would be bald in half a week if I sent the locks of hair I am asked for through the post every morning [...]

I lecture again at New York, Boston, Philadelphia, and other cities, so you see they understand and like me. All this sounds egotistical, but I do not like my friends in England to be ignorant of the success of one they have been so kind and loyal to.

And your supper – I should have been there. It must have been most dramatic. I am delighted about the Lily: she and I are facing great publics, and here I know she will succeed.

Phil writes me wonderful news of Katie, that she has ceased to be the modern Nero and is now angelic, and gives up to Gertie. If she does I no longer adore her: her fascinating villainy touched my artistic soul.

Please forgive my paper, and writing – they are characteristic of the country. But you were so good and kind to write. Pray remember me to Mr Lewis most affectionately, and believe me, ever sincerely yours

OSCAR WILDE

TL 94–95

2 **sybarite:** Sybarit (als Schlemmer verrufener Einwohner der antiken unteritalienischen Stadt Sybaris).
4 **to deluge s.o.:** jdn. überschwemmen.
5 **autograph:** Autogramm.
10 **egotistical:** von sich eingenommen, ichbezogen.
18 **angelic:** engelhaft.
19 **to adore:** verehren, anbeten.
20 **villainy:** Gemeinheit, Niedertracht.

Oscar Wilde photographed by W. & D. Downey, about 1894

In England, the arts that have escaped best are the arts in which the public take no interest. Poetry is an instance of what I mean. We have been able to have fine poetry in England because the public do not read it, and consequently do not influence it. The public like to insult poets because they are individual, but once they have insulted them, they leave them alone. In the case of the novel and the drama, arts in which the public do take an interest, the result of the exercise of popular authority has been absolutely ridiculous. No country produces such badly written fiction, such tedious, common work in the novel form, such silly, vulgar plays as England. […] Any attempt to extend the subject-matter of art is extremely distasteful to the public; and yet the vitality and progress of art depend in a large measure on the continual extension of subject-matter. The public dislike novelty because they are afraid of it. It represents to them a mode of Individualism, an assertion on the part of the artist that he selects his own subject, and treats it as he chooses. The public are quite right in their attitude. Art is Individualism, and Individualism is a disturbing and disintegrating force. Therein lies its immense value. For what it seeks to disturb is monotony of type, slavery of custom, tyranny of habit, and the reduction of man to the level of a machine. In Art, the public accept what has been, because they cannot alter it, not because they appreciate it. They swallow their classics whole, and never taste them. They endure them as the inevitable,

11 f. **tedious:** langweilig, öde.
12 **vulgar:** ordinär, geschmacklos.
14 **distasteful:** unangenehm, geschmacklos.

and as they cannot mar them, they mouth about them. Strangely enough, or not strangely, according to one's own views, this acceptance of the classics does a great deal of harm. The uncritical admiration of the Bible and Shakespeare in England is an instance of what I mean. *The Soul of Man under Socialism*; CW 1091–1092

To Mrs Bernard Beere

[17 April 1882] Kansas City, Missouri

My dear Bernie, I have lectured to the Mormons. The Opera House at Salt Lake is an enormous affair about the size of Covent Garden, and holds with ease fourteen families. They sit like this

and are very, very ugly. The President, a nice old man, sat with five wives in the stage box. I visited him in the afternoon and saw a charming daughter of his.

I have also lectured at Leadville, the great mining city in the Rocky Mountains. We took a whole day to get up to it on a narrow-gauge railway 14,000 feet in

1 **to mar:** verderben.
to mouth about s.th.: schwülstig von etwas reden.
9 **Mormons:** Mormonen (nordamerikanische Sekte).
14 **stage box:** Loge.
18 **narrow-gauge railway:** Schmalspurbahn.

height. My audience was entirely miners; their make-up excellent, red shirts and blonde beards, the whole of the first three rows being filled with McKee Rankins of every colour and dimension. I spoke to them of the early Florentines, and they slept as though no crime had ever stained the ravines of their mountain home. I described to them the pictures of Botticelli, and the name, which seemed to them like a new drink, roused them from their dreams, but when I told them in my boyish eloquence of the "secret of Botticelli" the strong men wept like children. Their sympathy touched me and I approached modern art and had almost won them over to a real reverence for what is beautiful when unluckily I described one of Jimmy Whistler's "nocturnes in blue and gold." Then they leaped to their feet and in their grand simple way swore that such things should not be. Some of the younger ones pulled their revolvers out and left hurriedly to see if Jimmy was "prowling about the saloons" or "wrastling a hash" at any eating shop. Had he been there I fear he would have been killed, their feeling was so bitter. Their enthusiasm satisfied me and I ended my lecture there. Then I found the Governor

1f. **make-up:** Aufzug, Erscheinungsbild.
6 **ravine:** Schlucht, Klamm.
7 **Botticelli:** Sandro B. (1445–1510), italienischer Maler.
9 **to rouse:** (auf)wecken.
10 **boyish:** jungenhaft.
eloquence: Wortgewandtheit, Beredtheit.
13 **reverence:** Ehrfurcht.
15 **nocturne:** Nachtstück.
19f. **to prowl about the saloons:** um die Kneipen streichen.
20 **to wrastle a hash:** einen Schlag verspachteln.

of the State waiting in a bullock *wagon* to bring me down the great silver-mine of the world, the Matchless. So off we drove, the miners carrying torches before us till we came to the shaft and were shot down in buckets (I of course true to my principle being graceful even in a bucket) and down in the great gallery of the mine, the walls and ceilings glittering with metal ore, was spread a banquet for us.

The amazement of the miners when they saw that art and appetite could go hand in hand knew no bounds; when I lit a long cigar they cheered till the silver fell in dust from the roof on our plates; and when I quaffed a cocktail without flinching, they unanimously pronounced me in their grand simple way "a bully boy with no glass eye" – artless and spontaneous praise which touched me more than the pompous panegyrics of literary critics ever did or could. Then I had to open a new vein, or lode, which with a silver drill I brilliantly performed, amidst unanimous

1 **bullock wagon:** Ochsenkarren.
3 **torch:** Fackel.
4 **shaft:** Schacht.
7 **to glitter:** glitzern.
metal ore: Silbererz.
8 **banquet:** Bankett, Festessen.
11 **bound:** Grenze.
13 **to quaff:** (Getränk) kippen.
without flinching: ohne mit der Wimper zu zucken.
13f. **unanimously** (adv.): einstimmig.
15 **a bully boy with no glass eye:** ein famoser Kumpel.
16f. **pompous:** schwülstig, bombastisch.
17 **panegyrics:** Lobeshymnen.
18 **lode:** Schacht.
19 **drill:** Bohrer.

applause. The silver drill was presented to me and the lode named "The Oscar." I had hoped that in their simple grand way they would have offered me shares in "The Oscar," but in their artless untutored fashion they did not. Only the silver drill remains as a memory of my night at Leadville.

I have had a delightful time all through California and Colorado and am now returning home, twice as affected as ever, my dear Bernie. Please remember me to dear Dot, to Reggie and all our mutual friends including Monty Morris, who won't write to me or even criticise me. Goodbye.

Your sincere friend OSCAR WILDE

TL 110–111

It is evident, then, that all authority in such things is bad. People sometimes inquire what form of government is most suitable for an artist to live under. To this question there is only one answer. The form of government that is most suitable to the artist is no government at all. Authority over him and his art is ridiculous. It has been stated that under despotism artists have produced lovely work. This is not quite so. Artists have visited despots, not as subjects to be tyrannised over, but as wandering wonder-makers, as fascinating vagrant personalities, to be entertained and charmed

4 **untutored:** ungeschult.
21 **despotism:** Despotismus, Gewaltherrschaft.
24 **wandering wonder-maker:** fahrender Wundertäter.
25 **vagrant:** vagabundierend.

and suffered to be at peace, and allowed to create. There is this to be said in favour of the despot, that he, being an individual, may have culture, while the mob, being a monster, has none. One who is an Emperor and King may stoop down to pick up a brush for a painter, but when the democracy stoops down it is merely to throw mud. And yet the democracy have not so far to stoop as the emperor. In fact, when they want to throw mud they have not to stoop at all. But there is no necessity to separate the monarch from the mob; all authority is equally bad.

The Soul of Man under Socialism; CW 1098–1099

To James McNeill Whistler

[Circa 23 February 1885]

Dear Butterfly, By the aid of a biographical dictionary I discovered that there were once two painters, called Benjamin West and Paul Delaroche, who recklessly took to lecturing on Art.

As of their works nothing at all remains, I conclude that they explained themselves away. Be warned in time, James; and remain, as I do, incomprehensible: to be great is to be misunderstood. *Tout à vous* OSCAR

3 **mob:** Pöbel.
4 **Emperor:** Kaiser.
5 **to stoop down:** sich bücken.
17 **recklessly** (adv.): leichtsinnig, gewagt.
21 **incomprehensible:** unverständlich.
22 **tout à vous** (Fr.): ganz der Ihre.

Private
Jimmy! You must *stamp* your letters – they are dear at twopence – and also do send them in proper time. 2.30 on Monday! *Ciel!* TL 170–171

To the Editor of the St James's Gazette

25 June [1890] 16 Tite Street

Sir, I have read your criticism of my story, *The Picture of Dorian Gray*, and I need hardly say that I do not propose to discuss its merits or demerits, its personalities or its lack of personality. England is a free country, and ordinary English criticism is perfectly free and easy. Besides, I must admit that, either from temperament or from taste, or from both, I am quite incapable of understanding how any work of art can be criticised from a moral standpoint. The sphere of art and the sphere of ethics are absolutely distinct and separate; and it is to the confusion between the two that we owe the appearance of Mrs Grundy, that amusing old lady who represents the only original form of humour that the middle classes of this country have been able to produce. What I do object to most strongly is that you should have placarded the town with posters on which was printed in large letters: MR OSCAR WILDE'S LATEST ADVERTISEMENT; A BAD CASE.

4 **le ciel** (Fr.): Himmel.
18 **Mrs Grundy:** Inbegriff der viktorianischen Engstirnigkeit und Prüderie.
22 **to placard:** plakatieren, mit Plakaten versehen.

Whether the expression "A Bad Case" refers to my book or to the present position of the Government, I cannot tell. What was silly and unnecessary was the use of the term "advertisement".

I think I may say without vanity – though I do not wish to appear to run vanity down – that of all men in England I am the one who requires least advertisement. I am tired to death of being advertised. I feel no thrill when I see my name in a paper. The chronicler does not interest me any more. I wrote this book entirely for my own pleasure, and it gave me very great pleasure to write it. Whether it becomes popular or not is a matter of absolute indifference to me. I am afraid, sir, that the real advertisement is your cleverly written article. The English public, as a mass, takes no interest in a work of art until it is told that the work in question is immoral, and your *réclame* will, I have no doubt, largely increase the sale of the magazine; in which sale, I may mention with some regret, I have no pecuniary interest.

I remain, sir, your obedient servant OSCAR WILDE

TL 257

5 **vanity:** Eitelkeit, Einbildung.
6 **to run s.th. down:** etwas anschwärzen, verunglimpfen.
9 **thrill:** Erregung.
chronicler: Chronist, Feuilletonist.
13 **indifference:** Gleichgültigkeit.
20 **pecuniary:** pekuniär, Geld-.

To the Editor of the Daily Chronicle

30 June [1890] 16 Tite Street

Sir, Will you allow me to correct some errors into which your critic has fallen in his review of my story, *The Picture of Dorian Gray*, published in today's issue of your paper?

Your critic states, to begin with, that I make desperate attempts to "vamp up" a moral in my story. Now, I must candidly confess that I do not know what "vamping" is. I see, from time to time, mysterious advertisements in the newspapers about "How to Vamp," but what vamping really means remains a mystery to me – a mystery that, like all other mysteries, I hope some day to explore.

However, I do not propose to discuss the absurd terms used by modern journalism. What I want to say is that, so far from wishing to emphasise any moral in my story, the real trouble I experienced in writing the story was that of keeping the extremely obvious moral subordinate to the artistic and dramatic effect.

When I first conceived the idea of a young man selling his soul in exchange for eternal youth – an idea that is old in the history of literature, but to which I have given new form – I felt that, from an aesthetic point of view, it would be difficult to keep the moral in its proper secondary place; and even now I do not feel

5 **issue:** Ausgabe (einer Zeitung).
8 **to vamp up:** aufschminken.
9 **candidly** (adv.): offen, freimütig.
20 **subordinate:** untergeordnet.
21 **to conceive the idea:** den Einfall haben.

quite sure that I have been able to do so. I think the moral too apparent. When the book is published in a volume I hope to correct this defect.

As for what the moral is, your critic states that it is this – that when a man feels himself becoming "too angelic" he should rush out and make a "beast of himself!" I cannot say that I consider this a moral. The real moral of the story is that all excess, as well as all renunciation, brings its punishment, and this moral is so far artistically and deliberately suppressed that it does not enunciate its law as a general principle, but realises itself purely in the lives of individuals, and so becomes simply a dramatic element in a work of art, and not the object of the work of art itself. TL 263

CARSON *(Counsel for the Defendant)*. Listen, sir. Here is one of the "Phrases and Philosophies for the Use of the Young" which you contributed: "Wickedness is a myth invented by good people to account for the curious attractiveness of others." You think that true?

WILDE. I rarely think that anything I write is true.

CARSON. Did you say "rarely"?

5f. **angelic:** engelhaft.
8f. **renunciation:** Selbstverleugnung.
11 **to enunciate:** (zu etwas) erklären.
15 **counsel for the defendant:** (Straf-)Verteidiger (des Marquess of Queensbury).
17 **wickedness:** Verdorbenheit.
18 **myth:** Mythos, Gerücht.
to account for s.th.: etwas begründen, erklären.

WILDE. I said "rarely." I might have said "never" – not true in the actual sense of the word.

CARSON. "Religions die when they are proved to be true." Is that true?

WILDE. Yes; I hold that. It is a suggestion towards a philosophy of the absorption of religions by science, but it is too big a question to go into now.

CARSON. Do you think that was a safe axiom to put forward for the philosophy of the young?

WILDE. Most stimulating.

CARSON. "If one tells the truth, one is sure, sooner or later, to be found out"?

WILDE. That is a pleasing paradox, but I do not set very high store on it as an axiom.

CARSON. Is it good for the young?

WILDE. Anything is good that stimulates thought in whatever age.

[…]

CARSON. After the criticisms that were passed on *Dorian Gray*, was it modified a good deal?

WILDE. No. Additions were made. In one case it was pointed out to me – not in a newspaper or anything of that sort, but by the only critic of the century whose opinion I set high, Mr. Walter Pater – that a certain passage was liable to misconstruction, and I made an addition.

6 **absorption:** Aufnahme, Integration.
8 **axiom:** Axiom, als absolut richtig anerkannter Grundsatz, gültige Wahrheit.
10 **to stimulate:** anregen.
13f. **to set very high store on s.th.:** etwas sehr hoch einschätzen.
24 **Pater:** Walter P. (1839–94), englischer Schriftsteller und Kritiker.
25 **liable to misconstruction:** missverständlich.

CARSON. This is in your introduction to *Dorian Gray*: "There is no such thing as a moral or an immoral book. Books are well written, or badly written." That expresses your view?

WILDE. My view on art, yes.

CARSON. Then, I take it, that no matter how immoral a book may be, if it is well written, it is, in your opinion, a good book?

WILDE. Yes, if it were well written so as to produce a sense of beauty, which is the highest sense of which a human being can be capable. If it were badly written, it would produce a sense of disgust.

CARSON. Then a well-written book putting forward perverted moral views may be a good book?

WILDE. No work of art ever puts forward views. Views belong to people who are not artists.

CARSON. A perverted novel might be a good book?

WILDE. I don't know what you mean by a "perverted" novel.

CARSON. Then I will suggest *Dorian Gray* as open to the interpretation of being such a novel?

WILDE. That could only be to brutes and illiterates. The views of Philistines on art are incalculably stupid.

CARSON. An illiterate person reading *Dorian Gray* might consider it such a novel?

WILDE. The views of illiterates on art are unaccount-

12 **disgust:** Ekel, Empörung.
17 **perverted:** pervertiert, verdorben.
22 **brute:** Ungebildeter, Rohling.
illiterate: Analphabet, Ungebildeter.
23 **Philistines:** Philister, Banausen.
incalculably (adv.): unberechenbar, unvorhersehbar.
26f. **unaccountable:** unerklärlich.

able. I am concerned only with my view of art. I don't care twopence what other people think of it.

CARSON. The majority of persons would come under your definition of Philistines and illiterates?

WILDE. I have found wonderful exceptions.

CARSON. Do you think that the majority of people live up to the position you are giving us?

WILDE. I am afraid they are not cultivated enough.

CARSON. Not cultivated enough to draw the distinction between a good book and a bad book?

WILDE. Certainly not.

CARSON. The affection and love of the artist of *Dorian Gray* might lead an ordinary individual to believe that it might have a certain tendency?

WILDE. I have no knowledge of the views of ordinary individuals.

CARSON. You did not prevent the ordinary individual from buying your book?

WILDE. I have never discouraged him. Tr 123–124

To Grant Richards

[June 1892] 16 Tite Street

Dear Sir, The new edition of my poems is limited to 200 copies, and these are meant not for reviewers, but merely for lovers of poetry, a small and quite unimportant sect of perfect people, so I fear I cannot bid

23 **reviewer:** Rezensent(in).
25 **sect:** Sekte; (fig.) Schule.

my book wander towards Mowbray House. Its raiment, gold smeared on tired purple, might attract attention in the Strand, and that would annoy it, books being delicate and most sensitive things, and, if they are books worth reading, having a strong dislike of the public.

So you see I must perforce refuse your request. Yours truly OSCAR WILDE

TL 304

To Leonard Smithers

Sunday [? 28 November 1897] Posilippo

Dear Smithers, Do try and make the Chiswick Press less mad and less maddening.

[…] It is really ridiculous that after my entire life has been wrecked by Society, people should still propose to exercise social tyranny over me, and try to force me to live in solitude – the one thing I can't stand. I lived in silence and solitude for two years in prison. I did not think that on my release my wife, my trustees, the guardians of my children, my few friends, such as they are, and my myriad enemies would combine to force

1f. **raiment:** Gewand, Einband.
2 **smeared:** verwischt, verlaufen.
tired: matt.
purple: Violett.
3 **the Strand:** nobler Londoner Stadtteil.
7 **perforce** (adv.): notgedrungen.
15 **wrecked:** zerstört.
17 **solitude:** Einsamkeit.
21 **myriad:** sehr große Menge.

me by starvation to live in silence and solitude again. After all in prison we had food of some kind: it was revolting, and made as loathsome as possible on purpose, and quite inadequate to sustain life in health. Still, there *was* food of some kind. The scheme now is that I am to live in silence and solitude and have no food at all. Really, the want of imagination in people is appalling. This scheme is put forward on moral grounds! It is proposed to leave me to die of starvation, or to blow my brains out in a Naples urinal. I never came across anyone in whom the moral sense was dominant who was not heartless, cruel, vindictive, log-stupid, and entirely lacking in the smallest sense of humanity. Moral people, as they are termed, are simple beasts. I would sooner have fifty unnatural vices than one unnatural virtue. It is unnatural virtue that makes the world, for those who suffer such a premature Hell. TL 686

1 **starvation:** Hungern, Aushungern.
2f. **revolting:** widerlich, ekelhaft.
3 **loathsome:** widerwärtig, abscheulich.
4 **inadequate:** unzulänglich, unzureichend.
7f. **appalling:** entsetzlich.
10 **Naples:** Neapel.
urinal: Pissoir.
12 **vindictive:** nachtragend, unversöhnlich.
log-stupid: strohdumm.
17 **premature:** vorzeitig.

VII

Body Count

GILBERT. The one duty we owe to history is to re-write it. That is not the least of the tasks in store for the critical spirit. When we have fully discovered the scientific laws that govern life, we shall realise that the one person who has more illusions than the dreamer is the man of action. He, indeed, knows neither the origin of his deeds nor their results. From the field in which he thought that he had sown thorns, we have gathered our vintage, and the fig-tree that he planted for our pleasure is as barren as the thistle, and more bitter. It is because Humanity has never known where it was going that it has been able to find its way. *The Critic as Artist*; CW 1023

4 (*to be*) **in store for s.th.:** auf etwas warten.
11 **thorn:** Dorn.
vintage: Weinernte, -lese.
11 f. **fig-tree:** Feigenbaum.
12 **barren:** unfruchtbar.
13 **thistle:** Distel.

And as he spake there came a great cry of mourning from the sea, even the cry that men hear when one of the Sea-folk is dead. And the young Fisherman leapt up, and left his wattled house, and ran down to the shore. And the black waves came hurrying to the shore, bearing with them a burden that was whiter than silver. White as the surf it was, and like a flower it tossed on the waves. And the surf took it from the waves, and the foam took it from the surf, and the shore received it, and lying at his feet the young Fisherman saw the body of the little Mermaid. Dead at his feet it was lying.

Weeping as one smitten with pain he flung himself down beside it, and he kissed the cold red of the mouth, and toyed with the wet amber of the hair. He flung himself down beside it on the sand, weeping as one trembling with joy, and in his brown arms he held it to his breast. Cold were the lips, yet he kissed them. Salt was the honey of the hair, yet he tasted it with a bitter joy. He kissed the closed eyelids, and the wild spray that lay upon their cups was less salt than his tears.

1 **spake** (arch.): *spoke.*
to mourn: trauern.
4 **wattled:** mit Stroh gedeckt.
7 **surf:** Brandung.
8 **to toss:** hin und her geworfen werden.
11 **mermaid:** Meerjungfrau.
13 **smitten with pain:** vom Schmerz gequält.
13f. **to fling o.s. down:** sich zu Boden werfen.
15 **amber:** Bernstein.
21 **spray:** Gischt.
cup: Wölbung.

And to the dead thing he made confession. Into the shells of its ears he poured the harsh wine of his tale. He put the little hands round his neck, and with his fingers he touched the thin reed of the throat. Bitter, bitter was his joy, and full of strange gladness was his pain.

The black sea came nearer, and the white foam moaned like a leper. With white claws of foam the sea grabbled at the shore. From the palace of the Sea-King came the cry of mourning again, and far out upon the sea the great Tritons blew hoarsely upon their horns.

"Flee away," said his Soul, "for ever doth the sea come nigher, and if thou tarriest it will slay thee. Flee away, for I am afraid, seeing that thy heart is closed against me by reason of the greatness of thy love. Flee away to a place of safety. Surely thou wilt not send me without a heart into another world?"

But the young Fisherman listened not to his Soul, but called on the little Mermaid and said, "Love is better than wisdom, and more precious than riches,

2 **harsh:** herb, bitter.
4 **reed:** Schilfrohr.
8 **leper:** Aussätzige(r).
claw: Kralle, Klaue.
9 **to grabble at s.th.:** nach etwas greifen.
11 **Triton:** Triton, niederer Meergott.
hoarsely (adv.): heiser.
12 **doth** (arch.): *does.*
13 **nigh:** nahe.
thou tarriest (arch.): *you tarry* (*to tarry:* bleiben, zögern).
to slay: töten.
thee (arch.): *you.*
14 **thy** (arch.): *your.*
16 **wilt** (arch.): *will.*

and fairer than the feet of the daughters of men. The fires cannot destroy it, nor can the waters quench it. I called on thee at dawn, and thou didst come to my call. The moon heard thy name, yet hadst thou no heed of me. For evilly had I left thee, and to my own hurt had I wandered away. Yet ever did thy love abide with me, and ever was it strong, nor did aught prevail against it, though I have looked upon evil and looked upon good. And now that thou art dead, surely I will die with thee also."

And his Soul besought him to depart, but he would not, so great was his love. And the sea came nearer, and sought to cover him with its waves, and when he knew that the end was at hand he kissed with mad lips the cold lips of the Mermaid, and the heart that was within him brake. And as through the fullness of his love his heart did break, the Soul found an entrance and entered in, and was one with him even as before. And the sea covered the young Fisherman with its waves.

And in the morning the Priest went forth to bless the sea, for it had been troubled. And with him went the monks and the musicians, and the candle-bearers, and the swingers of censers, and a great company.

And when the Priest reached the shore he saw the

2 **to quench:** löschen.
4 **to have heed of s.o.:** jdn. beachten.
7 **aught:** irgend etwas.
11 **to beseech:** anflehen, beschwören.
16 **brake:** *broke.*
24 **swingers of censers** (pl.): Weihrauchschwinger.

young Fisherman lying drowned in the surf, and clasped in his arms was the body of the little Mermaid. And he drew back frowning, and having made the sign of the Cross, he cried aloud and said, "I will not bless the sea nor anything that is in it. Accursed be the Sea-folk, and accursed be all they who traffic with them. And as for him who for love's sake forsook God, and so lieth here with his leman slain by God's judgment, take up his body and the body of his leman, and bury them in the corner of the Field of the Fullers, and set no mark above them, nor sign of any kind, that none may know the place of their resting. For accursed were they in their lives, and accursed shall they be in their deaths also."

And the people did as he commanded them, and in the corner of the Field of the Fullers, where no sweet herbs grew, they dug a deep pit, and laid the dead things within it.

And when the third year was over, and on a day that was a holy day, the Priest went up to the chapel, that he might show to the people the wounds of the Lord, and speak to them about the wrath of God.

And when he had robed himself with his robes, and

2 **to clasp s.o. in one's arms:** jdn. in die Arme schließen.
3 **to frown:** die Stirn runzeln.
5 **to accurse s.o.:** jdn. verfluchen.
6 **to traffic:** Umgang pflegen.
7 **to forsake:** verlassen.
8 **lieth** (arch.): *lies.*
leman: Buhle.
10 **Field of the Fullers:** Schindanger.
17 **herbs:** Kräuter.
22 **wrath:** Zorn.
23 **to robe o.s.:** sich ankleiden.

entered in and bowed himself before the altar, he saw that the altar was covered with strange flowers that never had been seen before. Strange were they to look at, and of curious beauty, and their beauty troubled him, and their odour was sweet in his nostrils, and he felt glad, and understood not why he was glad.

And after that he had opened the tabernacle, and incensed the monstrance that was in it, and shown the fair wafer to the people, and hid it again behind the veil of veils, he began to speak to the people, desiring to speak to them of the wrath of God. But the beauty of the white flowers troubled him, and their odour was sweet in his nostrils, and there came another word into his lips, and he spake not of the wrath of God, but of the God whose name is Love. And why he so spake, he knew not.

And when he had finished his word the people wept, and the Priest went back to his sacristy, and his eyes were full of tears. And the deacons came in and began to unrobe him, and took from him the alb and the girdle, the maniple and the stole. And he stood as one in a dream.

5 **odour:** Duft.
nostril: Nasenloch.
7 f. **to incense:** beweihräuchern.
9 **wafer:** Hostie.
10 **veil:** Schleier, Tuch, Vorhang.
18 **sacristy:** Sakristei.
19 **deacon:** Diakon.
20 **alb:** Albe, Messhemd.
21 **girdle:** Gürtel.
maniple: Manipel, Armstreifen des Messgewandes.
stole: Stola, Teil des Messgewandes.

And after that they had unrobed him, he looked at them and said, "What are the flowers that stand on the altar, and whence do they come?"

And they answered him, "What flowers they are we cannot tell, but they come from the corner of the Fullers' Field." And the Priest trembled, and returned to his own house and prayed.

And in the morning, while it was still dawn, he went forth with the monks and the musicians, and the candle-bearers and the swingers of censers, and a great company, and came to the shore of the sea, and blessed the sea, and all the wild things that are in it. The Fauns also he blessed, and the little things that dance in the woodland, and the bright-eyed things that peer through the leaves. All the things in God's world he blessed, and the people were filled with joy and wonder. Yet never again in the corner of the Fullers' Field grew flowers of any kind, but the field remained barren even as before. Nor came the Sea-folk into the bay as they had been wont to do, for they went to another part of the sea. *The Fisherman and His Soul*; CW 270–272

3 **whence:** woher.
13 **Faun:** Faun (Waldgeist).
15 **to peer:** starren, schielen, spähen.
19 **barren:** öde, unfruchtbar.
20 **to be wont to do s.th.:** gewöhnlich etwas tun, etwas zu tun pflegen.

Of all the rooms this was the brightest and the most beautiful. The walls were covered with a pink-flowered Lucca damask, patterned with birds and dotted with dainty blossoms of silver; the furniture was of massive silver, festooned with florid wreaths, and swinging Cupids; in front of the two large fireplaces stood great screens broidered with parrots and peacocks, and the floor, which was of sea-green onyx, seemed to stretch far away into the distance. Nor was he alone. Standing under the shadow of the doorway, at the extreme end of the room, he saw a little figure watching him. His heart trembled, a cry of joy broke from his lips, and he moved out into the sunlight. As he did so, the figure moved out also, and he saw it plainly.

The Infanta! It was a monster, the most grotesque monster he had ever beheld. Not properly shaped as all other people were, but hunchbacked, and crooked-

2 **pink-flowered:** rosa geblümt.
3 **Lucca:** italienische Stadt in der Toskana.
damask: Damast (einfarbiges Seidengewebe mit eingewebtem Muster).
dotted: gesprenkelt, übersät.
4 **dainty:** fein.
5 **to festoon s.th.:** etwas mit Girlanden behängen.
florid: blumig.
5f. **Cupid:** Amor (Liebesgott).
7 **broidered:** *embroidered:* bestickt.
parrot: Papagei.
peacock: Pfau.
8 **onyx:** Onyx (Mineral).
15 **Infanta:** Infantin (spanische Prinzessin).
16 **to behold:** erblicken.
17 **hunchbacked:** bucklig.
17f. **crooked-limbed:** verwachsen.

limbed, with huge lolling head and mane of black hair. The little Dwarf frowned, and the monster frowned also. He laughed, and it laughed with him, and held its hands to its sides, just as he himself was doing. He made it a mocking bow, and it returned him a low reverence. He went towards it, and it came to meet him, copying each step that he made, and stopping when he stopped himself. He shouted with amusement, and ran forward, and reached out his hand, and the hand of the monster touched his, and it was as cold as ice. He grew afraid, and moved his hand across, and the monster's hand followed it quickly. He tried to press on, but something smooth and hard stopped him. The face of the monster was now close to his own, and seemed full of terror. He brushed his hair off his eyes. It imitated him. He struck at it, and it returned blow for blow. He loathed it, and it made hideous faces at him. He drew back, and it retreated.

What is it? He thought for a moment, and looked round at the rest of the room. It was strange, but everything seemed to have its double in this invisible wall of clear water. Yes, picture for picture was repeated, and couch for couch. The sleeping Faun that lay in the alcove by the doorway had its twin brother

1 **to loll:** hin und her wackeln.
mane: Mähne.
2 **dwarf:** Zwerg.
to frown: die Stirn runzeln, finster blicken.
5 **mocking:** spöttisch.
5f. **reverence:** Gruß, Ehrerbietung.
17 **to loathe:** verabscheuen.
hideous: grässlich, abscheulich.
23 **Faun:** Faun (Waldgeist).

that slumbered, and the silver Venus that stood in the sunlight held out her arms to a Venus as lovely as herself.

Was it Echo? He had called to her once in the valley, and she had answered him word for word. Could she mock the eye, as she mocked the voice? Could she make a mimic world just like the real world? Could the shadows of things have colour and life and movement? Could it be that —?

He started, and taking from his breast the beautiful white rose, he turned round, and kissed it. The monster had a rose of its own, petal for petal the same! It kissed it with like kisses, and pressed it to its heart with horrible gestures.

When the truth dawned upon him, he gave a wild cry of despair, and fell sobbing to the ground. So it was he who was misshapen and hunchbacked, foul to look at and grotesque. He himself was the monster, and it was at him that all the children had been laughing, and the little Princess who he had thought loved him – she, too, had been merely mocking at his ugliness, and making merry over his twisted limbs. Why had they

1 **to slumber:** schlummern.
4 **Echo:** Nymphe der griechischen Mythologie.
6 **to mock:** nachmachen, -äffen; täuschen.
7 **mimic:** nachgeahmt.
10 **to start:** aufschrecken, zusammenfahren.
12 **petal:** Blütenblatt.
16 **to sob:** schluchzen.
17 **misshapen:** missgestaltet, unförmig.
foul: hässlich.
21 **to mock at s.th.:** etwas verspotten, sich über etwas lustig machen.
22 **twisted:** verkrümmt.

not left him in the forest, where there was no mirror to tell him how loathsome he was? Why had his father not killed him, rather than sell him to his shame? The hot tears poured down his cheeks, and he tore the white rose to pieces. The sprawling monster did the same, and scattered the faint petals in the air. It grovelled on the ground, and, when he looked at it, it watched him with a face drawn with pain. He crept away, lest he should see it, and covered his eyes with his hands. He crawled, like some wounded thing, into the shadow, and lay there moaning.

And at that moment the Infanta herself came in with her companions through the open window, and when they saw the ugly little Dwarf lying on the ground and beating the floor with his clenched hands, in the most fantastic and exaggerated manner, they went off into shouts of happy laughter, and stood all round him and watched him.

"His dancing was funny," said the Infanta; "but his acting is funnier still. Indeed, he is almost as good as the puppets, only, of course, not quite so natural." And she fluttered her big fan and applauded.

But the little Dwarf never looked up, and his sobs grew fainter and fainter, and suddenly he gave a curi-

2 **loathsome:** abscheulich.
5 **to sprawl:** ausgestreckt daliegen.
7 **to grovel:** kriechen.
8 **drawn with pain:** vor Schmerz verzerrt.
9 **lest:** damit nicht.
15 **to clench:** (Faust) ballen.
17 **to go off into laughter:** in Lachen ausbrechen.
21 **puppet:** Marionette, Puppe.
22 **to flutter s.th.:** schnell mit etwas schlagen.

ous gasp, and clutched his side. And then he fell back again, and lay quite still.

"That is capital," said the Infanta, after a pause; "but now you must dance for me."

"Yes," cried all the children, "you must get up and dance, for you are as clever as the Barbary apes, and much more ridiculous."

But the little Dwarf made no answer.

And the Infanta stamped her foot, and called out to her uncle, who was walking on the terrace with the Chamberlain, reading some despatches that had just arrived from Mexico, where the Holy Office had recently been established. "My funny little Dwarf is sulking," she cried, "you must wake him up, and tell him to dance for me."

They smiled at each other, and sauntered in, and Don Pedro stooped down, and slapped the Dwarf on the cheek with his embroidered glove. "You must dance," he said, "*petit monstre.* You must dance. The Infanta of Spain and the Indies wishes to be amused."

But the little Dwarf never moved.

"A whipping master should be sent for," said Don

1 **gasp:** Ringen nach Luft, Keuchen.
to clutch: umklammern.
6 **Barbary ape:** Berberäffchen.
11 **Chamberlain:** Kämmerer, Haushofmeister.
despatch: Depesche.
12 **Holy Office:** Inquisition.
13f. **to sulk:** schmollen, schlechter Laune sein.
16 **to saunter in:** hereinschlendern.
17 **to stoop down:** sich bücken.
to slap: schlagen, einen Klaps geben.
22 **whipping master:** Auspeitscher.

Pedro wearily, and he went back to the terrace. But the Chamberlain looked grave, and he knelt beside the little Dwarf, and put his hand upon his heart. And after a few moments he shrugged his shoulders, and rose up, and having made a low bow to the Infanta, he said –

"*Mi bella Princesa*, your funny little Dwarf will never dance again. It is a pity, for he is so ugly that he might have made the King smile."

"But why will he not dance again?" asked the Infanta, laughing.

"Because his heart is broken," answered the Chamberlain.

And the Infanta frowned, and her dainty rose-leaf lips curled in pretty disdain. "For the future let those who come to play with me have no hearts," she cried, and she ran out into the garden.

The Birthday of the Infanta; CW 245–247

Dorian Gray glanced at the picture, and suddenly an uncontrollable feeling of hatred for Basil Hallward came over him, as though it had been suggested to him by the image on the canvas, whispered into his ear by those grinning lips. The mad passions of a hunted animal stirred within him, and he loathed the man who was seated at the table, more than in his whole life he

4 **to shrug one's shoulders:** die Achseln zucken.
15 **disdain:** Verachtung, Hochmut.
22 **canvas:** Leinwand.
24 **to loathe:** verabscheuen.

had ever loathed anything. He glanced wildly around. Something glimmered on the top of the painted chest that faced him. His eye fell on it. He knew what it was. It was a knife that he had brought up, some days before, to cut a piece of cord, and had forgotten to take away with him. He moved slowly towards it, passing Hallward as he did so. As soon as he got behind him, he seized it, and turned round. Hallward stirred in his chair as if he was going to rise. He rushed at him, and dug the knife into the great vein that is behind the ear, crushing the man's head down on the table, and stabbing again and again.

There was a stifled groan, and the horrible sound of someone choking with blood. Three times the outstretched arms shot up convulsively, waving grotesque stiff-fingered hands in the air. He stabbed him twice more, but the man did not move. Something began to trickle on the floor. He waited for a moment, still pressing the head down. Then he threw the knife on the table, and listened.

He could hear nothing but the drip, drip on the threadbare carpet. He opened the door and went out on the landing. The house was absolutely quiet. No one was about. For a few seconds he stood bending

2 **to glimmer:** glänzen, schwach schimmern.
11f. **to stab:** (zu)stechen.
13 **stifled groan:** ersticktes Stöhnen.
14 **to choke:** ersticken, würgen.
15 **convulsively** (adv.): krampfhaft.
18 **to trickle:** tropfen, sickern.
22 **threadbare:** fadenscheinig.
23 **landing:** Treppenabsatz.

over the balustrade, and peering down into the black seething well of darkness. Then he took out the key and returned to the room, locking himself in as he did so.

The thing was still seated in the chair, straining over the table with bowed head, and humped back, and long fantastic arms. Had it not been for the red jagged tear in the neck, and the clotted black pool that was slowly widening on the table, one would have said that the man was simply asleep.

How quickly it had all been done!

The Picture of Dorian Gray; CW 122–123

GILL *(Counsel for the Crown)*. Where did you first meet Wilde?

PARKER. Taylor asked us to visit him (Taylor) next day at Little College Street. We went the next morning. He said he could introduce us to a man who was good for plenty of money, and that we were to meet him (Taylor) at the St. James's bar. We went the next evening to the St. James's and saw Taylor there. He took us to a restaurant in Rupert Street. I think it was the Solferino. We were shown upstairs to a pri-

1 **to peer:** spähen, starren.
2 **to seethe:** kochen, brodeln.
5 **to strain:** gekrümmt liegen, sich krümmen.
6 **humped:** gebeugt, gekrümmt.
7 **jagged:** gezackt.
8 **clotted:** klumpig, geronnen.
13 **counsel for the crown:** Staatsanwalt.

vate room, in which there was a dinner table laid for four. After a while Wilde came in and I was formally introduced. I had never seen him before, but I had heard of him. We dined about eight o'clock. We all four sat down to dinner, Wilde sitting on my left.

GILL. Who made the fourth?

PARKER. My brother, William Parker. I had promised Taylor that he should accompany me.

GILL. Was the dinner a good dinner?

PARKER. Yes. The table was lighted with red-shaded candles. We had plenty of champagne with our dinner and brandy and coffee afterwards. We all partook of it. Wilde paid for the dinner.

GILL. Of what nature was the conversation?

PARKER. General, at first. Nothing was then said as to the purposes for which we had come together.

GILL. And then?

PARKER. Subsequently Wilde said to me, "This is the boy for me! Will you go to the Savoy Hotel with me?" I consented, and Wilde drove me in a cab to the hotel. Only he and I went, leaving my brother and Taylor behind. At the Savoy we went first to Wilde's sitting room on the second floor.

GILL. More drink was offered you there?

PARKER. Yes, we had liqueurs. Wilde then asked me to go into his bedroom with him.

GILL. Let us know what occurred there?

13f. **to partake of s.th.:** an etwas teilhaben.
19 **subsequently** (adv.): später, anschließend.
21 **to consent:** zustimmen, einwilligen.
26 **liqueur:** Likör.

PARKER. He committed the act of sodomy upon me.

GILL. With your consent?

(Witness did not reply.)

GILL. Did Wilde give you any money on that occasion?

PARKER. Before I left Wilde gave me £ 2, telling me to call at the Savoy Hotel in a week. I went there about a week afterwards at eleven o'clock at night. We had supper, with champagne. Wilde on that occasion committed the same acts as on the first occasion. I stayed about two hours. Tr 192–193

Everything about my tragedy has been hideous, mean, repellent, lacking in style. Our very dress makes us grotesques. We are the zanies of sorrow. We are clowns whose hearts are broken. We are specially designed to appeal to the sense of humour. On November 13th 1895 I was brought down here from London. From two o'clock till half-past two on that day I had to stand on the centre platform of Clapham Junction in convict dress and handcuffed, for the world to look at. I had been taken out of the Hospital Ward without a moment's notice being given to me. Of all possible objects I was the most grotesque. When people saw me they laughed. Each train as it came up swelled the audience.

1 **sodomy:** Homosexualität.
11 **hideous:** grässlich, abscheulich.
12 **repellent:** abstoßend.
13 **zany:** Witzfigur.
18 **junction:** Knotenpunkt, Umsteigebahnhof.
19 **handcuffed:** in Handschellen.
20 **hospital ward:** Krankenstation.

Nothing could exceed their amusement. That was of course before they knew who I was. As soon as they had been informed, they laughed still more. For half an hour I stood there in the grey November rain surrounded by a jeering mob.

For a year after that was done to me I wept every day at the same hour and for the same space of time. That is not such a tragic thing as possibly it sounds to you. To those who are in prison, tears are a part of every day's experience. A day in prison on which one does not weep is a day on which one's heart is hard, not a day on which one's heart is happy.

De Profundis; CW 936–937

To the Editor of the Daily Chronicle

27 May [1897] [Dieppe]

[…]

On Saturday week last I was in my cell at about one o'clock occupied in cleaning and polishing the tins I had been using for dinner. Suddenly I was startled by the prison silence being broken by the most horrible and revolting shrieks, or rather howls, for at first I thought some animal like a bull or a cow was being un-

5 **to jeer:** johlen.
mob: Pöbel, Menschenmenge.
19 **to startle s.o.:** jdn. auf-, erschrecken.
21 **revolting:** widerlich.
shriek: lauter, schriller (Angst-, Schmerzens-)Schrei.
howl: Heulen, Geheul.
22f. **unskilfully** (adv.): ungeschickt.

skilfully slaughtered outside the prison walls. I soon realised, however, that the howls proceeded from the basement of the prison, and I knew that some wretched man was being flogged. I need not say how hideous and terrible it was for me, and I began to wonder who it was who was being punished in this revolting manner. Suddenly it dawned upon me that they might be flogging this unfortunate lunatic. My feelings on the subject need not be chronicled; they have nothing to do with the question.

The next day, Sunday 16th, I saw the poor fellow at exercise, his weak, ugly, wretched face bloated by tears and hysteria almost beyond recognition. He walked in the centre ring along with the old men, the beggars, and the lame people, so that I was able to observe him the whole time. It was my last Sunday in prison, a perfectly lovely day, the finest day we had had the whole year, and there, in the beautiful sunlight, walked this poor creature – made once in the image of God – grinning like an ape, and making with his hands the most fantastic gestures, as though he was playing in the air on some invisible stringed instrument, or arranging and dealing counters in some curious game. All the

4 **to flog s.o.:** jdn. auspeitschen, prügeln, schlagen.
5 **hideous:** grässlich, abscheulich.
8 **lunatic:** Geistesgestörter.
9 **to chronicle s.th.:** etwas (in zeitlicher Abfolge) aufzeichnen, berichten.
11 f. **at exercise:** beim Rundgang.
12 **bloated:** geschwollen, aufgedunsen.
20 **ape:** Affe.
22 **invisible:** unsichtbar.
stringed instrument: Saiteninstrument.

while these hysterical tears, without which none of us ever saw him, were making soiled runnels on his white swollen face. The hideous and deliberate grace of his gestures made him like an antic. He was a living grotesque. The other prisoners all watched him, and not one of them smiled. Everybody knew what had happened to him, and that he was being driven insane – was insane already. After half an hour he was ordered in by the warder, and I suppose punished. At least he was not at exercise on Monday, though I think I caught sight of him at the corner of the stone-yard, walking in charge of a warder.

[…]

His number is, or was, A.2.II. I also managed to find out his name. It is Prince. Something should be done at once for him. He is a soldier, and his sentence is one of court-martial. The term is six months. Three have yet to run. May I ask you to use your influence to have this case examined into, and to see that the lunatic prisoner is properly treated?

No report of the Medical Commissioners is of any avail. It is not to be trusted. The medical inspectors do not seem to understand the difference between idiocy and lunacy – between the entire absence of a function or organ and the diseases of a function or organ. This

2 **runnel:** Rinne, Spur.
4 **antic:** Narr, Possenreißer.
7 **insane:** verrückt, wahnsinnig.
9 **warder:** Gefängnisaufseher.
17 **court-martial:** Kriegsgericht.
21 f. **of avail:** von Nutzen.
23 **idiocy:** Schwachsinn.
24 **lunacy:** Wahnsinn.

man A.2.II will, I have no doubt, be able to tell his name, the nature of his offence, the day of the month, the date of the beginning and expiration of his sentence, and answer any ordinary simple question; but that his mind is diseased admits of no doubt. At present it is a horrible duel between himself and the doctor. The doctor is fighting for a theory. The man is fighting for his life. I am anxious that the man should win. TL 573–574

3 **expiration:** Ablauf, Ende.

Oscar Wilde photographed by Cameron, 1889

VIII

News from Limbo

The Doer of Good

It was night-time and He was alone.

And he saw afar-off the walls of a round city and went towards the city.

And when He came near He heard within the city the tread of the feet of joy, and the laughter of the mouth of gladness and the loud noise of many lutes. And He knocked at the gate and certain of the gate-keepers opened to Him.

And He beheld a house that was of marble and had fair pillars of marble before it. The pillars were hung with garlands, and within and without there were torches of cedar. And He entered the house.

And when He had passed through the hall of chalcedony and the hall of jasper, and reached the long hall

5 **afar-off:** in der Ferne.
9 **lute:** Laute.
10f. **gate-keeper:** Torhüter.
12 **to behold:** erblicken.
14 **garland:** Girlande.
15 **torch:** Fackel.
cedar: Zeder(nholz).
16f. **chalcedony:** Chalzedon (Mineral).
17 **jasper:** Jaspis (Mineral).
17f. **hall of feasting:** Festsaal.

of feasting, He saw lying on a couch of sea-purple one whose hair was crowned with red roses and whose lips were red with wine.

And He went behind him and touched him on the shoulder and said to him, “Why do you live like this?”

And the young man turned round and recognised Him, and made answer and said, “But I was a leper once, and you healed me. How else should I live?”

And He passed out of the house and went again into the street.

And after a little while He saw one whose face and raiment were painted and whose feet were shod with pearls. And behind her came, slowly as a hunter, a young man who wore a cloak of two colours. Now the face of the woman was as the fair face of an idol, and the eyes of the young man were bright with lust.

And He followed swiftly and touched the hand of the young man and said to him, “Why do you look at this woman and in such wise?”

And the young man turned round and recognised Him and said, “But I was blind once, and you gave me sight. At what else should I look?”

And He ran forward and touched the painted raiment of the woman and said to her, “Is there no other way in which to walk save the way of sin?”

And the woman turned round and recognised Him,

1 **sea-purple:** purpurfarbig wie das Meer.
7 **leper:** Aussätziger.
12 **raiment:** Gewand.
shod: Part. Perf. von *to shoe:* beschuhen, beschlagen.
14 **cloak:** Umhang, Mantel.
15 **idol:** Abgott.
16 **lust:** sinnliche Begierde.

and laughed and said, "But you forgave me my sins, and the way is a pleasant way."

And He passed out of the city.

And when He had passed out of the city He saw seated by the roadside a young man who was weeping.

And He went towards him and touched the long locks of his hair and said to him, "Why are you weeping?"

And the young man looked up and recognised Him and made answer, "But I was dead once and you raised me from the dead. What else should I do but weep?"

CW 863–864

At nine o'clock the next morning his servant came in with a cup of chocolate on a tray, and opened the shutters. Dorian was sleeping quite peacefully, lying on his right side, with one hand underneath his cheek. He looked like a boy who had been tired out with play, or study.

The man had to touch him twice on the shoulder before he awoke, and as he opened his eyes a faint smile passed across his lips, as though he had been lost in some delightful dream. Yet he had not dreamed at all. His night had been untroubled by any images of pleasure or of pain. But youth smiles without any reason. It is one of its chiefest charms.

He turned round, and, leaning upon his elbow,

15 **shutter:** Fensterladen.

began to sip his chocolate. The mellow November sun came streaming into the room. The sky was bright, and there was a genial warmth in the air. It was almost like a morning in May.

Gradually the events of the preceding night crept with silent blood-stained feet into his brain, and reconstructed themselves there with terrible distinctness. He winced at the memory of all that he had suffered, and for a moment the same curious feeling of loathing for Basil Hallward that had made him kill him as he sat in the chair, came back to him, and he grew cold with passion. The dead man was still sitting there, too, and in the sunlight now. How horrible that was! Such hideous things were for the darkness, not for the day.

He felt that if he brooded on what he had gone through he would sicken or grow mad. There were sins whose fascination was more in the memory than in the doing of them; strange triumphs that gratified the pride more than the passions, and gave to the intellect a quickened sense of joy, greater than any joy they brought, or could ever bring, to the senses. But this was not one of them. It was a thing to be driven out of

1 **to sip:** in kleinen Schlucken trinken, schlürfen.
mellow: mild.
6 **blood-stained:** blutbefleckt.
8 **to wince:** zusammenzucken.
9 **loathing:** Abscheu.
14 **hideous:** grässlich, abscheulich.
16 **to brood on s.th.:** über etwas grübeln.
19 **to gratify:** befriedigen.
21 **quickened:** gesteigert, verstärkt.

the mind, to be drugged with poppies, to be strangled lest it might strangle one itself.

[...]

The suspense became unbearable. Time seemed to him to be crawling with feet of lead, while he by monstrous winds was being swept towards the jagged edge of some black cleft of precipice. He knew what was waiting for him there; saw it indeed, and, shuddering, crushed with dank hands his burning lids as though he would have robbed the very brain of sight, and driven the eyeballs back into their cave. It was useless. The brain had its own food on which it battened, and the imagination, made grotesque by terror, twisted and distorted as a living thing by pain, danced like some foul puppet on a stand, and grinned through moving masks. Then, suddenly, Time stopped for him. Yes: that blind, slow-breathing thing crawled no more, and horrible thoughts, Time being dead, raced nimbly on in front, and dragged a hideous future from its grave, and showed it to him. He stared at it. Its very horror made him stone.

The Picture of Dorian Gray; CW 125–128

1 **poppy:** Mohn.
1f. **to strangle s.th.:** etwas ersticken, abwürgen, unterdrücken.
2 **lest:** damit nicht.
5 **lead:** Blei.
6 **jagged:** gezackt, zerklüftet.
7 **cleft:** Schlund.
precipice: Abgrund.
9 **dank:** feucht.
11 **cave:** Augenhöhle.
12 **to batten on s.th.:** sich an etwas gütlich tun.
15 **puppet:** Marionette.
18 **nimbly** (adv.): flink, hurtig.

HEROD. What is this miracle of the daughter of Jairus?

FIRST NAZARENE. The daughter of Jairus was dead. He raised her from the dead.

HEROD. He raises the dead?

FIRST NAZARENE. Yea, sire, He raiseth the dead.

HEROD. I do not wish Him to do that. I forbid Him to do that. I allow no man to raise the dead. This Man must be found and told that I forbid Him to raise the dead. Where is this Man at present?

SECOND NAZARENE. He is in every place, my lord, but it is hard to find Him.

FIRST NAZARENE. It is said that He is now in Samaria.

A JEW. It is easy to see that this is not Messias, if He is in Samaria. It is not to the Samaritans that Messias shall come. The Samaritans are accursed. They bring no offerings to the Temple.

SECOND NAZARENE. He left Samaria a few days since. I think that at the present moment He is in the neighbourhood of Jerusalem.

FIRST NAZARENE. No, he is not there. I have just come from Jerusalem. For two months they have had no tidings of Him.

HEROD. No matter! But let them find Him, and tell Him from me, I will not allow him to raise the dead! To change water into wine, to heal the lepers and the blind … He may do these things if He will. I say

6 **raiseth** (arch.): *raises*.
16 **accursed:** verflucht.
23 **tidings** (pl.): Nachricht.
26 **leper:** Aussätzige(r).

nothing against these things. In truth I hold it a good deed to heal a leper. But I allow no man to raise the dead. It would be terrible if the dead came back.

Salomé; CW 565

To the Home Secretary

2 July 1896 H.M. Prison, Reading

To the Right Honourable Her Majesty's Principal Secretary of State for the Home Department.

The Petition of the above-named prisoner humbly sheweth that he does not desire to attempt to palliate in any way the terrible offences of which he was rightly found guilty, but to point out that such offences are forms of sexual madness and are recognised as such not merely by modern pathological science but by much modern legislation, notably in France, Austria, and Italy, where the laws affecting these misdemeanours have been repealed, on the ground that they are diseases to be cured by a physician, rather than crimes to be punished by a judge. In the works of eminent men of science such as Lombroso and Nordau, to take merely

8 **Home Department:** Innenministerium.
10 **sheweth** (arch.): *shows.*
to palliate: beschönigen.
14 **pathological science:** Krankheitslehre.
15 **legislation:** Gesetzgebung.
16 **misdemeanour:** Delikt.
17 **to repeal s.th.:** etwas für ungültig erklären, aufheben.
19 **eminent:** hervorragend, berühmt.

two instances out of many, this is specially insisted on with reference to the intimate connection between madness and the literary and artistic temperament, Professor Nordau in his book on "Degenerescence" published in 1894 having devoted an entire chapter to the petitioner as a specially typical example of this fatal law.

The petitioner is now keenly conscious of the fact that while the three years preceding his arrest were from the intellectual point of view the most brilliant years of his life (four plays from his pen having been produced on the stage with immense success, and played not merely in England, America, and Australia, but in almost every European capital, and many books that excited much interest at home and abroad having been published), still that during the entire time he was suffering from the most horrible form of erotomania, which made him forget his wife and children, his high social position in London and Paris, his European distinction as an artist, the honour of his name and family, his very humanity itself, and left him the helpless prey of the most revolting passions, and of a gang of people who for their own profit ministered to them, and then drove him to his hideous ruin.

It is under the ceaseless apprehension lest this insan-

2 **intimate:** innig.
4 **degenerescence:** Entartung.
16f. **erotomania:** Erotomanie, Liebeswahnsinn.
21 **prey:** Beute.
revolting: widerlich, ekelhaft.
23 **hideous:** grässlich, abscheulich.
24 **ceaseless:** unaufhörlich.
lest: dass.
24f. **insanity:** Wahnsinn, Geisteskrankheit.

ity, that displayed itself in monstrous sexual perversion before, may now extend to the entire nature and intellect, that the petitioner writes this appeal which he earnestly entreats may be at once considered. Horrible as all actual madness is, the terror of madness is no less appalling, and no less ruinous to the soul.

For more than thirteen dreadful months now, the petitioner has been subject to the fearful system of solitary cellular confinement: without human intercourse of any kind; without writing materials whose use might help to distract the mind: without suitable or sufficient books, so essential to any literary man, so vital for the preservation of mental balance: condemned to absolute silence: cut off from all knowledge of the external world and the movements of life: [...].

For more than a year the petitioner's mind has borne this. It can bear it no longer. He is quite conscious of the approach of an insanity that will not be confined to one portion of the nature merely, but will extend over all alike, and his desire, his prayer is that his sentence may be remitted now, so that he may be taken abroad by his friends and may put himself under medical care so that the sexual insanity from which he suffers may be cured. He knows only too well that his career as a dramatist and writer is ended, and his name

4 **to entreat:** dringend bitten, ersuchen.
6 **to appal:** erschrecken, entsetzen.
9 **solitary cellular confinement:** Einzelhaft.
9f. **human intercourse:** soziale Kontakte.
11 **to distract:** ablenken, zerstreuen.
22 **to remit s.th.:** etwas erlassen, aufheben.

blotted from the scroll of English Literature never to be replaced: that his children cannot bear that name again, and that an obscure life in some remote country is in store for him: he knows that, bankruptcy having come upon him, poverty of a most bitter kind awaits him, and that all the joy and beauty of existence is taken from him for ever: but at least in all his hopelessness he still clings to the hope that he will not have to pass directly from the common gaol to the common lunatic asylum. TL 401–404

There are few of us who have not sometimes wakened before dawn, either after one of those dreamless nights that make us almost enamoured of death, or one of those nights of horror and misshapen joy, when through the chambers of the brain sweep phantoms more terrible than reality itself, and instinct with that vivid life that lurks in all grotesques, and that lends to Gothic art its enduring vitality, this art being, one might fancy, especially the art of those whose minds

1 **to blot s.th.:** etwas tilgen.
scroll: Verzeichnis, Annalen.
3 **obscure:** unerkannt, unbedeutend.
4 **to be in store for s.o.:** auf jdn. warten, jdm. bevorstehen.
bankruptcy: Zahlungsunfähigkeit, Bankrott.
9 **gaol:** Gefängnis.
10 **lunatic asylum:** Irrenanstalt.
13 **to make s.o. enamoured of s.th.:** jdn. in etwas verliebt machen.
14 **misshapen:** entstellt.
17 **to lurk:** lauern, verborgen liegen.

have been troubled with the malady of reverie. Gradually white fingers creep through the curtains, and they appear to tremble. In black fantastic shapes, dumb shadows crawl into the corners of the room, and crouch there. Outside, there is the stirring of birds among the leaves, or the sound of men going forth to their work, or the sigh and sob of the wind coming down from the hills, and wandering round the silent house, as though it feared to wake the sleepers, and yet must needs call forth sleep from her purple cave. Veil after veil of thin dusky gauze is lifted, and by degrees the forms and colours of things are restored to them, and we watch the dawn remaking the world in its antique pattern. The wan mirrors get back their mimic life. The flameless tapers stand where we had left them, and beside them lies the half-cut book that we had been studying, or the wired flower that we had worn at the ball, or the letter that we had been afraid to read, or that we had read too often. Nothing seems to us changed. Out of the unreal shadows of the night comes back the real life that we had known. We have

1 **malady:** (schleichende) Krankheit.
reverie: Träumerei.
5 **to crouch:** sich kauern, hocken.
7 **sob:** Schluchzen.
10 **needs** (adv.): unbedingt, notwendigerweise.
purple: purpurn; violett.
veil: Schleier.
11 **dusky:** dämmrig, düster.
gauze: Gaze, feiner Nebel.
14 **wan:** glanzlos, trüb.
mimic: mimisch; nachgemacht.
15 **taper:** Wachskerze.
17 **wired:** mit einem Stützdrähtchen versehen.

to resume it where we had left off, and there steals over us a terrible sense of the necessity for the continuance of energy in the same wearisome round of stereotyped habits, or a wild longing, it may be, that our eyelids might open some morning upon a world that had been refashioned anew in the darkness for our pleasure, a world in which things would have fresh shapes and colours, and be changed, or have other secrets, a world in which the past would have little or no place, or survive, at any rate, in no conscious form of obligation or regret, the remembrance even of joy having its bitterness, and the memories of pleasure their pain.

The Picture of Dorian Gray; CW 104–105

I was a man who stood in symbolic relations to the art and culture of my age. I had realised this for myself at the very dawn of my manhood, and had forced my age to realise it afterwards. Few men hold such a position in their own lifetime and have it so acknowledged. It is usually discerned, if discerned at all, by the historian, or the critic, long after both the man and his age have passed away. With me it was different. I felt it myself, and made others feel it. Byron was a symbolic figure, but his relations were to the passion of his age and its

3 **wearisome:** ermüdend.
4 **stereotyped habits:** eingefleischte Gewohnheiten.
6 **to refashion s.th.:** etwas umgestalten.
11 **remembrance:** Erinnerung.
19 **to discern:** wahrnehmen, erkennen, feststellen.
22 **Byron:** George Gordon Noël, Lord B. (1788–1824), englischer Dichter.

weariness of passion. Mine were to something more noble, more permanent, of more vital issue, of larger scope.

The gods had given me almost everything. I had genius, a distinguished name, high social position, brilliancy, intellectual daring: I made art a philosophy, and philosophy an art: I altered the minds of men and the colours of things: there was nothing I said or did that did not make people wonder: I took the drama, the most objective form known to art, and made it as personal a mode of expression as the lyric or the sonnet, at the same time that I widened its range and enriched its characterisation: drama, novel, poem in rhyme, poem in prose, subtle or fantastic dialogue, whatever I touched I made beautiful in a new mode of beauty: to truth itself I gave what is false no less than what is true as its rightful province, and showed that the false and the true are merely forms of intellectual existence. I treated Art as the supreme reality, and life as a mere mode of fiction: I awoke the imagination of my century so that it created myth and legend around me: I summed up all systems in a phrase, and all existence in an epigram.

Along with these things, I had things that were different. I let myself be lured into long spells of senseless and sensual ease. I amused myself with being a *flâneur*,

2 **issue:** Bedeutung, Gewicht.
12 **to enrich:** bereichern.
19 **supreme:** höchste(r, s).
21 **myth:** Mythos.
23 **epigram:** Epigramm, kurzes Sinngedicht.
25 **to lure s.o. into s.th.:** jdn. zu etwas verlocken, verführen.
26 **le flâneur** (Fr.): Müßiggänger.

a dandy, a man of fashion. I surrounded myself with the smaller natures and the meaner minds. I became the spendthrift of my own genius, and to waste an eternal youth gave me a curious joy. Tired of being on the heights I deliberately went to the depths in the search for new sensations. What the paradox was to me in the sphere of thought, perversity became to me in the sphere of passion. Desire, at the end, was a malady, or a madness, or both. I grew careless of the lives of others. I took pleasure where it pleased me and passed on. I forgot that every little action of the common day makes or unmakes character, and that therefore what one has done in the secret chamber one has some day to cry aloud on the housetops. I ceased to be Lord over myself. I was no longer the Captain of my Soul, and did not know it. I allowed you to dominate me, and your father to frighten me. I ended in horrible disgrace.

De Profundis; CW 912–913

Where there is Sorrow there is holy ground. Some day you will realise what that means. You will know nothing of life till you do. Robbie, and natures like his, can realise it. When I was brought down from my prison to the Court of Bankruptcy between two policemen, Robbie waited in the long dreary corridor,

3 **spendthrift:** Verschwender.
8 **malady:** (schleichende) Krankheit.
17f. **disgrace:** Schande, Ehrlosigkeit.
23 **bankruptcy:** Bankrott, Insolvenz.
24 **dreary:** düster, trostlos.

that before the whole crowd, whom an action so sweet and simple hushed into silence, he might gravely raise his hat to me, as handcuffed and with bowed head I passed him by. Men have gone to heaven for smaller things than that. It was in this spirit, and with this mode of love that the saints knelt down to wash the feet of the poor, or stooped to kiss the leper on the cheek. I have never said one single word to him about what he did. I do not know to the present moment whether he is aware that I was even conscious of his action. It is not a thing for which one can render formal thanks in formal words. I store it in the treasury-house of my heart. I keep it there as a secret debt that I am glad to think I can never possibly repay. It is embalmed and kept sweet by the myrrh and cassia of many tears. When Wisdom has been profitless to me, and Philosophy barren, and the proverbs and phrases of those who have sought to give me consolation as dust and ashes in my mouth, the memory of that little lowly silent act of Love has unsealed for me all the wells of pity, made the desert blossom like a rose, and brought me out of the bitterness of lonely exile into harmony with the wounded, broken and great heart of the world. *De Profundis*; CW 906

2 **to hush s.o. into silence:** jdn. zum Verstummen bringen
3 **handcuffed:** in Handschellen.
7 **to stoop:** sich niederbeugen.
leper: Aussätzige(r).
12f. **treasury-house:** Schatzkammer
14f. **to embalm s.th.** (fig.): etwas vor der Vergessenheit bewahren.
15 **myrrh and cassia:** Myrrhe und Zimt(rinde).
17 **barren:** unfruchtbar.
20 **lowly:** bescheiden.
to unseal: öffnen.

I now see that sorrow, being the supreme emotion of which man is capable, is at once the type and test of all great Art.

[…]

I remember talking once on this subject to one of the most beautiful personalities I have ever known: a woman, whose sympathy and noble kindness to me both before and since the tragedy of my imprisonment have been beyond power and description: one who has really assisted me, though she does not know it, to bear the burden of my troubles more than anyone else in the whole world has: and all through the mere fact of her existence: through her being what she is, partly an ideal and partly an influence, a suggestion of what one might become, as well as a real help towards becoming it, a soul that renders the common air sweet, and makes what is spiritual seem as simple and natural as sunlight or the sea, one for whom Beauty and Sorrow walk hand in hand and have the same message. On the occasion of which I am thinking I recall distinctly how I said to her that there was enough suffering in one narrow London lane to show that God did not love man, and that wherever there was any sorrow, though but that of a child in some little garden weeping over a fault that it had or had not committed, the whole face of creation was completely marred. I was entirely wrong. She told me so, but I could not believe her. I was not in the sphere in which such belief was to

1 **supreme:** höchste(r, s).
20 **to recall:** sich erinnern.
26 **to mar s.th.:** etwas entstellen.

be attained to. Now it seems to me that Love of some kind is the only possible explanation of the extraordinary amount of suffering that there is in the world. I cannot conceive any other explanation. I am convinced that there is no other, and that if the worlds have indeed, as I have said, been built out of Sorrow, it has been by the hands of Love, because in no other way could the Soul of man for whom the worlds are made reach the full stature of its perfection. Pleasure for the beautiful body, but Pain for the beautiful Soul.

De Profundis; CW 919–921

To Robert Ross

Tuesday [Postmark 16 August 1898] [Postmark Paris]

My dear Robbie, I have been suffering from a complete paralysis of epistolary power. I simply have not been able to write to anyone.

[…]

Thanks very much for your suggestion to let me have my income weekly: it is the only thing to do. I must however leave my hotel, and really live as a very poor man. My hotel bill for rooms and *café-au-lait* is 100 francs a month. I must try and get rooms for 40 francs instead of 70. I don't think I shall ever really

1 **to attain s.th.:** etwas erlangen, erreichen.
4 **to conceive:** sich vorstellen, denken.
15 **paralysis:** Lähmung.
epistolary: Briefe oder das Schreiben von Briefen betreffend.

write again. Something is killed in me. I feel no desire to write. I am unconscious of power. Of course my first year in prison destroyed me body and soul. It could not have been otherwise.

I saw Cossie Lennox with his wife and Harry Melvill the other night. Cossie and Harry Melvill both cut me! I felt as if I had been cut by two Piccadilly renters. For people whom one has had to give themselves moral or social airs is childish. I was very much hurt. But have quite recovered.

Give my love to dear Reggie. That harvest-moon, Eugene, loomed on me on the Boulevard the other day. He looked like a prize melon. TL 759–760

To the Rev. J. Page Hopps

14 January 1885

Dear Mr Hopps, I am very sorry to say that I am confined to the house with a severe cold, caught by lecturing in a Lincolnshire snowstorm, and am not allowed by my doctor to travel. It is with much regret that I find myself unable to join in the meeting tomorrow, as I sympathise most strongly with the object in question. The present style of burying and sorrowing for the dead seems to me to make grief grotesque, and to turn

7 **renter:** Strichjunge.
11 **harvest-moon:** Vollmond.
13 **prize melon:** preisgekrönte Riesenmelone.
14 **Rev.:** Abk. von *Reverend*.
16f. **to be confined to s.th.:** an etwas gefesselt, auf etwas beschränkt sein.

mourning to a mockery. Any reform you can bring about in these customs would be of value quite inestimable. The present ostentation and extravagance of burial rites seems to me to harmonise but ill with the real feeling of those at the doors of whose house the Angel of Death has knocked. The ceremony by which we part from those whom we have loved should not merely be noble in its meaning, but simple in its sincerity. [...] If we are to have funeral memorials at all, far better models are to be found in the beautiful crosses of Ireland, such as the cross at Monasterboice, or in the delicate bas-reliefs on Greek tombs. Above all, such art, if we are to have it, should concern itself more with the living than the dead – should be rather a noble symbol for the guiding of life than an idle panegyric on those who are gone. If a man needs an elaborate tombstone in order to remain in the memory of his country, it is clear that his living at all was an act of absolute superfluity. Keats's grave is a hillock of green grass with a plain headstone, and is to me the holiest

1 **mourning:** Trauer.
mockery: Gespött.
2f. **inestimable:** unschätzbar.
3 **ostentation:** (protzige) Zurschaustellung.
4 **burial rites:** Beisetzungsrituale.
8f. **sincerity:** Aufrichtigkeit, Echtheit.
12 **bas-relief:** Flachrelief.
tomb: Grab.
15f. **panegyric:** Loblied.
17 **tombstone:** Grabstein.
19 **superfluity:** Überfluss.
Keats: John K. (1795–1821), englischer Dichter.
hillock: kleiner Hügel.
20 **headstone:** Kopfstein.

place in Rome. There is in Westminster Abbey a periwigged admiral in a nightgown hurried off to heaven by two howling cherubs, which is one of the best examples I know of ostentatious obscurity.

TL 168–169

1f. **periwigged:** mit Perücke.
2 **nightgown:** Nachthemd.
3 **to howl:** heulen.
cherub: Cherub, Engel.
4 **ostentatious obscurity:** nichtige Großtuerei.

IX

Saint Oscar

And the end of it all is that I have got to forgive you. I must do so. I don't write this letter to put bitterness into your heart, but to pluck it out of mine. For my own sake I must forgive you. One cannot always keep an adder in one's breast to feed on one, nor rise up every night to sow thorns in the garden of one's soul. It will not be difficult at all for me to do so, if you help me a little. Whatever you did to me in old days I always readily forgave. It did you no good then. Only one whose life is without stain of any kind can forgive sins. But now when I sit in humiliation and disgrace it is different. My forgiveness should mean a great deal to you now. Some day you will realise it. Whether you do so early or late, soon or not at all, my way is clear before me. I cannot allow you to go through life bearing in your heart the burden of having ruined a man like me. The thought might make you callously indif-

7 **adder:** Natter, Viper.
8 **thorn:** Dorn.
12 **without stain:** makellos.
13 **humiliation:** Erniedrigung, Demütigung.
disgrace: Schande.
19 **callously** (adv.): gefühllos, abgestumpft.
19f. **indifferent:** gleichgültig.

ferent, or morbidly sad. I must take the burden from you and put it on my own shoulders.

I must say to myself that neither you nor your father, multiplied a thousand times over, could possibly have ruined a man like me: that I ruined myself: and that nobody, great or small, can be ruined except by his own hand. I am quite ready to do so. I am trying to do so, though you may not think it at the present moment. If I have brought this pitiless indictment against you, think what an indictment I bring without pity against myself. Terrible as what you did to me was, what I did to myself was far more terrible still.

De Profundis; CW 912

The House of Judgment

And there was silence in the House of Judgment, and the Man came naked before God.

And God opened the Book of the Life of the Man.

And God said to the Man, "Thy life hath been evil, and thou hast shown cruelty to those who were in need of succour, and to those who lacked help thou hast been bitter and hard of heart. The poor called to thee

1 **morbidly** (adv.): krankhaft.
9 **pitiless:** mitleidlos.
indictment: Anklage.
18 **thy** (arch.): *your*.
19 **thou hast** (arch.): *you have*.
20 **succour:** Hilfe, Beistand.
21 **thee** (arch.): *you*.

Caricature of Oscar Wilde by Max Beerbohm, 1894

and thou didst not hearken, and thine ears were closed to the cry of My afflicted. The inheritance of the fatherless thou didst take unto thyself, and thou didst send the foxes into the vineyard of thy neighbour's field. Thou didst take the bread of the children and give it to the dogs to eat, and My lepers who lived in the marshes, and were at peace and praised Me, thou didst drive forth on to the highways, and on Mine earth out of which I made thee thou didst spill innocent blood."

And the Man made answer and said, "Even so did I."

And again God opened the Book of the Life of the Man.

And God said to the Man, "Thy life hath been evil, and the Beauty I have shown thou hast sought for, and the Good I have hidden thou didst pass by. The walls of thy chamber were painted with images, and from the bed of thine abominations thou didst rise up to the sound of flutes. Thou didst build seven altars to the sins I have suffered, and didst eat of the thing that may not be eaten, and the purple of thy raiment was broi-

1 **to hearken:** hören.
thine (arch.): *your*.
2 **afflicted:** niedergeschlagen, bedrückt.
4 **vineyard:** Weinberg.
6 **leper:** Aussätziger.
7 **marsh:** Sumpfland, Moor.
9 **to spill:** vergießen.
19 **abomination:** Schande, Schändlichkeit.
20 **flute:** Flöte.
22 **purple:** Purpur.
raiment: Gewand.
22f. **broidered:** *embroidered:* bestickt.

dered with the three signs of shame. Thine idols were neither of gold nor of silver that endure, but of flesh that dieth. Thou didst stain their hair with perfumes and put pomegranates in their hands. Thou didst stain their feet with saffron and spread carpets before them. With antimony thou didst stain their eyelids and their bodies thou didst smear with myrrh. Thou didst bow thyself to the ground before them, and the thrones of thine idols were set in the sun. Thou didst show to the sun thy shame and to the moon thy madness."

And the Man made answer and said, "Even so did I."

And a third time God opened the Book of the Life of the Man.

And God said to the Man, "Evil hath been thy life, and with evil didst thou requite good, and with wrong-doing kindness. The hands that fed thee thou didst wound, and the breasts that gave thee suck thou didst despise. He who came to thee with water went away thirsting, and the outlawed men who hid thee in their tents at night thou didst betray before dawn. Thine enemy who spared thee thou didst snare in an ambush,

1 **idol:** Götzenbild.
3 **dieth** (arch.): *dies.*
4 **pomegranate:** Granatapfel.
5 **saffron:** Safran.
6 **antimony:** Spießglanz (Halbmetall).
16 **to requite:** vergelten.
19 **to despise:** verachten.
20 **outlawed:** geächtet, gesetzlos.
21 **to betray:** verraten.
22 **to snare:** eine Falle stellen.
ambush: Hinterhalt.

and the friend who walked with thee thou didst sell for a price, and to those who brought thee Love thou didst ever give Lust in thy turn."

And the Man made answer and said, "Even so did I."

And God closed the Book of the Life of the Man, and said, "Surely I will send thee into Hell. Even into Hell will I send thee."

And the Man cried out, "Thou canst not."

And God said to the Man, "Wherefore can I not send thee to Hell, and for what reason?"

"Because in Hell have I always lived," answered the Man.

And there was silence in the House of Judgment.

And after a space God spake, and said to the Man, "Seeing that I may not send thee into Hell, surely I will send thee unto Heaven. Even unto Heaven will I send thee."

And the Man cried out, "Thou canst not."

And God said to the Man, "Wherefore can I not send thee unto Heaven, and for what reason?"

"Because never, and in no place, have I been able to imagine it," answered the Man.

And there was silence in the House of Judgment.

CW 865–866

3 **lust:** sinnliche Begierde.

The Artist

One evening there came into his soul the desire to fashion an image of *The Pleasure that abideth for a Moment.* And he went forth into the world to look for bronze. For he could only think in bronze.

But all the bronze of the whole world had disappeared, nor anywhere in the whole world was there any bronze to be found, save only the bronze of the image of *The Sorrow that endureth for Ever.*

Now this image he had himself, and with his own hands, fashioned, and had set it on the tomb of the one thing he had loved in life. On the tomb of the dead thing he had most loved had he set this image of his own fashioning, that it might serve as a sign of the love of man that dieth not, and a symbol of the sorrow of man that endureth for ever. And in the whole world there was no other bronze save the bronze of this image.

And he took the image he had fashioned, and set it in a great furnace, and gave it to the fire.

And out of the bronze of the image of *The Sorrow that endureth for Ever* he fashioned an image of *The Pleasure that abideth for a Moment.* CW 863

3 **abideth** (arch.): *abides.*
11 **tomb:** Grab.
20 **furnace:** Schmelzofen.

GILBERT. [...] It is a strange thing, this transference of emotion. We sicken with the same maladies as the poets, and the singer lends us his pain. Dead lips have their message for us, and hearts that have fallen to dust can communicate their joy. We run to kiss the bleeding mouth of Fantine, and we follow Manon Lescaut over the whole world. Ours is the love-madness of the Tyrian, and the terror of Orestes is ours also. There is no passion that we cannot feel, no pleasure that we may not gratify, and we can choose the time of our initiation and the time of our freedom also. Life! Life! Don't let us go to life for our fulfilment or our experience. It is a thing narrowed by circumstances, incoherent in its utterance, and without that fine correspondence of form and spirit which is the only thing that can satisfy the artistic and critical temperament. It makes us pay too high a price for its wares, and we purchase the meanest of its secrets at a cost that is monstrous and infinite.

ERNEST. Must we go, then, to Art for everything?

GILBERT. For everything. Because Art does not hurt us.

1 **transference:** Übertragung.
2 **to sicken with s.th.:** an etwas erkranken.
malady: (schleichende) Krankheit.
6 **Fantine:** Figur aus *Les Misérables* (1862), einem Roman des französischen Schriftstellers Victor Hugo (1802–85).
6f. **Manon Lescaut:** Titelfigur eines Romans (1731) des französischen Schriftstellers Antoine François Prévost d'Exiles (1697–1763).
8 **Tyrian:** Einwohner der phönizischen Stadt Tyrus.
Orestes: Gestalt der griechischen Mythologie.
10 **to gratify:** befriedigen, stillen.
11 **initiation:** Einführung, Einleitung.
14 **incoherent:** zusammenhangslos.
18 **ware:** Ware.

The tears that we shed at a play are a type of the exquisite sterile emotions that it is the function of Art to awaken. We weep, but we are not wounded. We grieve, but our grief is not bitter. In the actual life of man, sorrow, as Spinoza says somewhere, is a passage to a lesser perfection. But the sorrow with which Art fills us both purifies and initiates, if I may quote once more from the great art critic of the Greeks. It is through Art, and through Art only, that we can realise our perfection; through Art, and through Art only, that we can shield ourselves from the sordid perils of actual existence. This results not merely from the fact that nothing that one can imagine is worth doing, and that one can imagine everything, but from the subtle law that emotional forces, like the forces of the physical sphere, are limited in extent and energy. One can feel so much, and no more. And how can it matter with what pleasure life tries to tempt one, or with what pain it seeks to maim and mar one's soul, if in the spectacle of the lives of those who have never existed one has found the true secret of joy, and wept away one's tears over their deaths who, like Cordelia and the daughter of Brabantio, can never die?

The Critic as Artist; CW 1038

5 **Spinoza:** Baruch S. (1632–77), niederländischer Philosoph.
7 **to purify:** reinigen.
12 **sordid:** scheußlich.
peril: Gefahr.
15 **subtle:** geheimnisvoll.
20 **to maim:** verstümmeln.
to mar: verderben.
23 **Cordelia:** Figur in Shakespeares *King Lear*.
24 **Brabantio:** Figur in Shakespeares *Othello*.

To Carlos Blacker

12 July 1897 [Chalet Bourgeat] Berneval-sur-Mer

My dear old Friend, I need not tell you with what feelings of affection and gratitude I read your letter. You were always my staunch friend and stood by my side for many years.

[…] I learnt many things in prison that were terrible to learn, but I learnt some good lessons that I needed. I learnt gratitude: and though, in the eyes of the world, I am of course a disgraced and ruined man, still every day I am filled with wonder at all the beautiful things that are left to me: loyal and loving friends: good health: books, one of the greatest of the many worlds God has given to each man: the pageant of the seasons: the loveliness of leaf and flower: the nights hung with silver and the dawns dim with gold. I often find myself strangely happy. You must not think of me as being morbidly sad, or wilfully living in sadness, that sin which Dante punishes so terribly. My desire to live is as intense as ever, and though my heart is broken, hearts are made to be broken: that is why God sends sorrow into the world. The hard heart is the evil thing of life and of art. I have also learnt sympathy with suffering. To me, suffering seems now a sacramental

5 **staunch:** *stanch:* treu, zuverlässig.
10 **disgraced:** entehrt.
14 **pageant:** Schauspiel.
16 **dim:** matt.
18 **morbidly** (adv.): krankhaft.
wilfully (adv.): eigensinnig, willentlich.
24 **sacramental:** feierlich, heilig.

thing, that makes those whom it touches holy. I think I am in many respects a much better fellow than I was, and I now make no more exorbitant claims on life: I accept everything. I am sure it is all right. TL 621

3 **exorbitant:** übertrieben, übermäßig.

Sketch of Oscar Wilde by Henri de Toulouse-Lautrec

X

Prince Paradox or How to Demolish a Monument

The Happy Prince

High above the city, on a tall column, stood the statue of the Happy Prince. He was gilded all over with thin leaves of fine gold, for eyes he had two bright sapphires, and a large red ruby glowed on his sword-hilt.

He was very much admired indeed. "He is as beautiful as a weathercock," remarked one of the Town Councillors who wished to gain a reputation for having artistic tastes; "only not quite so useful," he added, fearing lest people should think him unpractical, which he really was not.

"Why can't you be like the Happy Prince?" asked a sensible mother of her little boy who was crying for the moon. "The Happy Prince never dreams of crying for anything."

6 **gilded:** vergoldet.
7f. **sapphire:** Saphir.
8 **ruby:** Rubin.
to glow: glühen.
sword-hilt: Schwertgriff, Heft.
10 **weathercock:** Wetterhahn.
10f. **Town Councillor:** Stadtrat, Ratsherr.
13 **lest:** dass.

"I am glad there is some one in the world who is quite happy," muttered a disappointed man as he gazed at the wonderful statue.

"He looks just like an angel," said the Charity Children as they came out of the cathedral in their bright scarlet cloaks and their clean white pinafores.

"How do you know?" said the Mathematical Master, "you have never seen one."

"Ah! but we have, in our dreams," answered the children; and the Mathematical Master frowned and looked very severe, for he did not approve of children dreaming.

One night there flew over the city a little Swallow. His friends had gone away to Egypt six weeks before, but he had stayed behind, for he was in love with the most beautiful Reed. He had met her early in the spring as he was flying down the river after a big yellow moth, and had been so attracted by her slender waist that he had stopped to talk to her.

"Shall I love you?" said the Swallow, who liked to come to the point at once, and the Reed made him a low bow. So he flew round and round her, touching the water with his wings, and making silver ripples. This was his courtship, and it lasted all through the summer.

2 **to mutter:** murmeln.
2f. **to gaze at s.th.:** etwas anstarren, -staunen.
4f. **Charity Children:** Kinder in der Armenschule.
6 **scarlet:** scharlachrot.
cloak: Mantel.
pinafore: Schürze.
10 **to frown:** die Stirn runzeln.
16 **reed:** Schilfrohr.
23 **ripples:** kleine Wellen.
24 **courtship:** (Liebes-)Werbung.

"It is a ridiculous attachment," twittered the other Swallows; "she has no money, and far too many relations;" and indeed the river was quite full of Reeds. Then, when the autumn came they all flew away.

After they had gone he felt lonely, and began to tire of his lady-love. "She has no conversation," he said, "and I am afraid that she is a coquette, for she is always flirting with the wind." And certainly, whenever the wind blew, the Reed made the most graceful curtseys. "I admit that she is domestic," he continued, "but I love travelling, and my wife, consequently, should love travelling also."

"Will you come away with me?" he said finally to her, but the Reed shook her head, she was so attached to her home.

"You have been trifling with me," he cried. "I am off to the Pyramids. Good-bye!" and he flew away.

All day long he flew, and at night-time he arrived at the city. "Where shall I put up?" he said; "I hope the town has made preparations."

Then he saw the statue on the tall column.

"I will put up there," he cried; "it is a fine position, with plenty of fresh air." So he alighted just between the feet of the Happy Prince.

"I have a golden bedroom," he said softly to himself as he looked round, and he prepared to go to sleep; but just as he was putting his head under his wing a large drop of water fell on him. "What a curious

1 **to twitter:** zwitschern.
7 **coquette:** Kokette, gefallsüchtige Frau.
9f. **curtsey:** Knicks.
16 **to trifle:** spielen, tändeln, flirten.
23 **to alight:** sich niederlassen.

thing!" he cried; "there is not a single cloud in the sky, the stars are quite clear and bright, and yet it is raining. The climate in the north of Europe is really dreadful. The Reed used to like the rain, but that was merely her selfishness."

Then another drop fell.

"What is the use of a statue if it cannot keep the rain off?" he said; "I must look for a good chimney-pot," and he determined to fly away.

But before he had opened his wings, a third drop fell, and he looked up, and saw – Ah! what did he see?

The eyes of the Happy Prince were filled with tears, and tears were running down his golden cheeks. His face was so beautiful in the moonlight that the little Swallow was filled with pity.

"Who are you?" he said.

"I am the Happy Prince."

"Why are you weeping then?" asked the Swallow; "you have quite drenched me."

"When I was alive and had a human heart," answered the statue, "I did not know what tears were, for I lived in the Palace of Sans-Souci, where sorrow is not allowed to enter. In the daytime I played with my companions in the garden, and in the evening I led the dance in the Great Hall. Round the garden ran a very lofty wall, but I never cared to ask what lay beyond it, everything about me was so beautiful. My courtiers

5 **selfishness:** Selbstsucht.
8 **chimney-pot:** Schornsteinaufsatz.
19 **to drench:** durchnässen.
22 **Sans-Souci** (Fr.): sprechender Name; wörtl.: ohne Sorge.
26 **lofty:** hoch.
27 **courtier:** Höfling.

called me the Happy Prince, and happy indeed I was, if pleasure be happiness. So I lived, and so I died. And now that I am dead they have set me up here so high that I can see all the ugliness and all the misery of my city, and though my heart is made of lead yet I cannot choose but weep."

"What! is he not solid gold?" said the Swallow to himself. He was too polite to make any personal remarks out loud.

"Far away," continued the statue in a low musical voice, "far away in a little street there is a poor house. One of the windows is open, and through it I can see a woman seated at a table. Her face is thin and worn, and she has coarse, red hands, all pricked by the needle, for she is a seamstress. She is embroidering passion-flowers on a satin gown for the loveliest of the Queen's maids-of-honour to wear at the next Court-ball. In a bed in the corner of the room her little boy is lying ill. He has a fever, and is asking for oranges. His mother has nothing to give him but river water, so he is crying. Swallow, Swallow, little Swallow, will you not bring her the ruby out of my sword-hilt? My feet are fastened to this pedestal and I cannot move."

"I am waited for in Egypt," said the Swallow. "My friends are flying up and down the Nile, and talking to the large lotus-flowers. Soon they will go to sleep in

5 **lead:** Blei.
14 **pricked:** zerstochen.
15 **seamstress:** Näherin.
to embroider: sticken.
16 **gown:** Gewand, Kleid.
17 **maid-of-honour:** Hofdame.
23 **pedestal:** Sockel.

the tomb of the great King. The King is there himself in his painted coffin. He is wrapped in yellow linen, and embalmed with spices. Round his neck is a chain of pale green jade, and his hands are like withered leaves."

"Swallow, Swallow, little Swallow," said the Prince, "will you not stay with me for one night, and be my messenger? The boy is so thirsty, and the mother so sad."

"I don't think I like boys," answered the Swallow. "Last summer, when I was staying on the river, there were two rude boys, the miller's sons, who were always throwing stones at me. They never hit me, of course; we swallows fly far too well for that, and besides, I come of a family famous for its agility; but still, it was a mark of disrespect."

But the Happy Prince looked so sad that the little Swallow was sorry. "It is very cold here," he said; "but I will stay with you for one night, and be your messenger."

"Thank you, little Swallow," said the Prince.

So the Swallow picked out the great ruby from the Prince's sword, and flew away with it in his beak over the roofs of the town.

He passed by the cathedral tower, where the white

1 **tomb:** Grab.
2 **linen:** Leinen.
3 **to embalm s.o.:** jdn. einbalsamieren, salben.
spice: Spezerei.
4 **to wither:** (ver)welken, trocknen.
15 **agility:** Behendigkeit.
16 **mark of disrespect:** Zeichen mangelnder Achtung.
23 **beak:** Schnabel.

marble angels were sculptured. He passed by the palace and heard the sound of dancing. A beautiful girl came out on the balcony with her lover. "How wonderful the stars are," he said to her, "and how wonderful is the power of love!"

"I hope my dress will be ready in time for the State-ball," she answered; "I have ordered passion-flowers to be embroidered on it; but the seamstresses are so lazy."

He passed over the river, and saw the lanterns hanging to the masts of the ships. He passed over the Ghetto, and saw the old Jews bargaining with each other, and weighing out money in copper scales. At last he came to the poor house and looked in. The boy was tossing feverishly on his bed, and the mother had fallen asleep, she was so tired. In he hopped, and laid the great ruby on the table beside the woman's thimble. Then he flew gently round the bed, fanning the boy's forehead with his wings. "How cool I feel!" said the boy, "I must be getting better:" and he sank into a delicious slumber.

Then the Swallow flew back to the Happy Prince, and told him what he had done. "It is curious," he remarked, "but I feel quite warm now, although it is so cold."

"That is because you have done a good action," said

1 **to sculpture s.th.:** etwas meißeln, in Stein hauen.
10 **lantern:** Laterne.
13 **copper scale:** kupferne Waagschale.
15 **to toss:** sich hin und her werfen, wälzen.
16 **to hop:** hüpfen.
18 **thimble:** Fingerhut.

the Prince. And the little Swallow began to think, and then he fell asleep. Thinking always made him sleepy.

When day broke he flew down to the river and had a bath. "What a remarkable phenomenon!" said the Professor of Ornithology as he was passing over the bridge. "A swallow in winter!" And he wrote a long letter about it to the local newspaper. Every one quoted it, it was full of so many words that they could not understand.

"To-night I go to Egypt," said the Swallow, and he was in high spirits at the prospect. He visited all the public monuments, and sat a long time on top of the church steeple. Wherever he went the Sparrows chirruped, and said to each other, "What a distinguished stranger!" so he enjoyed himself very much.

When the moon rose he flew back to the Happy Prince. "Have you any commissions for Egypt?" he cried; "I am just starting."

"Swallow, Swallow, little Swallow," said the Prince, "will you not stay with me one night longer?"

"I am waited for in Egypt," answered the Swallow. "To-morrow my friends will fly up to the Second Cataract. The river-horse couches there among the bulrushes, and on a great granite house sits the God Memnon. All night long he watches the stars, and

5 **ornithology:** Vogelkunde.
11 **in high spirits:** frohgemut.
13 **church steeple:** Kirchturm.
13 f. **to chirrup:** zwitschern.
22 f. **cataract:** (großer) Wasserfall.
23 **to couch:** versteckt liegen.
23 f. **bulrush:** Rohrkolben.
25 **Memnon:** kolossale Sitzfigur im altägyptischen Theben.

when the morning star shines he utters one cry of joy, and then he is silent. At noon the yellow lions come down to the water's edge to drink. They have eyes like green beryls, and their roar is louder than the roar of the cataract."

"Swallow, Swallow, little Swallow," said the Prince, "far away across the city I see a young man in a garret. He is leaning over a desk covered with papers, and in a tumbler by his side there is a bunch of withered violets. His hair is brown and crisp, and his lips are red as a pomegranate, and he has large and dreamy eyes. He is trying to finish a play for the Director of the Theatre, but he is too cold to write any more. There is no fire in the grate, and hunger has made him faint."

"I will wait with you one night longer," said the Swallow, who really had a good heart. "Shall I take him another ruby?"

"Alas! I have no ruby now," said the Prince; "my eyes are all that I have left. They are made of rare sapphires, which were brought out of India a thousand years ago. Pluck out one of them and take it to him. He will sell it to the jeweller, and buy firewood, and finish his play."

"Dear Prince," said the Swallow, "I cannot do that"; and he began to weep.

"Swallow, Swallow, little Swallow," said the Prince, "do as I command you."

4 **beryl:** Beryll (Edelstein).
7 **garret:** Dachstube.
9 **tumbler:** Wasserglas.
10 **crisp:** kraus, lockig.
11 **pomegranate:** Granatapfel.
14 **grate:** Feuerrost.

So the Swallow plucked out the Prince's eye, and flew away to the student's garret. It was easy enough to get in, as there was a hole in the roof. Through this he darted, and came into the room. The young man had his head buried in his hands, so he did not hear the flutter of the bird's wings, and when he looked up he found the beautiful sapphire lying on the withered violets.

"I am beginning to be appreciated," he cried; "this is from some great admirer. Now I can finish my play," and he looked quite happy.

The next day the Swallow flew down to the harbour. He sat on the mast of a large vessel and watched the sailors hauling big chests out of the hold with ropes. "Heave a-hoy!" they shouted as each chest came up. "I am going to Egypt!" cried the Swallow, but nobody minded, and when the moon rose he flew back to the Happy Prince.

"I am come to bid you good-bye," he cried.

"Swallow, Swallow, little Swallow," said the Prince, "will you not stay with me one night longer?"

"It is winter," answered the Swallow, "and the chill snow will soon be here. In Egypt the sun is warm on the green palm-trees, and the crocodiles lie in the mud and look lazily about them. My companions are building a nest in the Temple of Baalbec, and the pink and

4 **to dart:** fliegen, schnellen.
14 **to haul:** heben, hieven.
hold: Lade-, Frachtraum.
22 **chill:** kalt, eisig.
26 **Baalbec:** Baalbek, Stadt im heutigen Libanon mit bedeutendem Tempelbezirk aus der Römerzeit.

white doves are watching them, and cooing to each other. Dear Prince, I must leave you, but I will never forget you, and next spring I will bring you back two beautiful jewels in place of those you have given away. The ruby shall be redder than a red rose, and the sapphire shall be as blue as the great sea."

"In the square below," said the Happy Prince, "there stands a little match-girl. She has let her matches fall in the gutter, and they are all spoiled. Her father will beat her if she does not bring home some money, and she is crying. She has no shoes or stockings, and her little head is bare. Pluck out my other eye, and give it to her, and her father will not beat her."

"I will stay with you one night longer," said the Swallow, "but I cannot pluck out your eye. You would be quite blind then."

"Swallow, Swallow, little Swallow," said the Prince, "do as I command you."

So he plucked out the Prince's other eye, and darted down with it. He swooped past the match-girl, and slipped the jewel into the palm of her hand. "What a lovely bit of glass!" cried the little girl; and she ran home, laughing.

Then the Swallow came back to the Prince. "You are blind now," he said, "so I will stay with you always."

"No, little Swallow," said the poor prince, "you must go away to Egypt."

1 **to coo:** gurren.
8 **match-girl:** Streichholzverkäuferin.
9 **gutter:** Gosse.
20 **to swoop past s.o.:** an jdm. vorbeischießen, -sausen.

"I will stay with you always," said the Swallow, and he slept at the Prince's feet.

All the next day he sat on the Prince's shoulder, and told him stories of what he had seen in strange lands. He told him of the red ibises, who stand in long rows on the banks of the Nile, and catch goldfish in their beaks; of the Sphinx, who is as old as the world itself, and lives in the desert, and knows everything; of the merchants, who walk slowly by the side of their camels and carry amber beads in their hands; of the King of the Mountains of the Moon, who is as black as ebony, and worships a large crystal; of the great green snake that sleeps in a palm-tree, and has twenty priests to feed it with honey-cakes; and of the pygmies who sail over a big lake on large flat leaves, and are always at war with the butterflies.

"Dear little Swallow," said the Prince, "you tell me of marvellous things, but more marvellous than anything is the suffering of men and of women. There is no Mystery so great as Misery. Fly over my city, little Swallow, and tell me what you see there."

So the Swallow flew over the great city, and saw the rich making merry in their beautiful houses, while the beggars were sitting at the gates. He flew into dark lanes, and saw the white faces of starving children looking out listlessly at the black streets. Under the archway of a bridge two little boys were lying in one

5 **ibis:** Ibis (storchähnlicher Vogel).
10 **amber:** Bernstein.
11 **ebony:** Ebenholz.
14 **pygmy:** Pygmäe; Zwerg.
26 **listlessly** (adv.): teilnahmslos.
27 **archway:** Bogen(gang).

another's arms to try and keep themselves warm. "How hungry we are!" they said. "You must not lie here," shouted the watchman, and they wandered out into the rain.

Then he flew back and told the Prince what he had seen.

"I am covered with fine gold," said the Prince, "you must take it off, leaf by leaf, and give it to my poor; the living always think that gold can make them happy."

Leaf after leaf of the fine gold the Swallow picked off, till the Happy Prince looked quite dull and grey. Leaf after leaf of the fine gold he brought to the poor, and the childrens' faces grew rosier, and they laughed and played games in the street. "We have bread now!" they cried.

Then the snow came, and after the snow came the frost. The streets looked as if they were made of silver, they were so bright and glistening; long icicles like crystal daggers hung down from the eaves of the houses, everybody went about in furs, and the little boys wore scarlet caps and skated on the ice.

The poor little Swallow grew colder and colder, but he would not leave the Prince, he loved him too well. He picked up crumbs outside the baker's door when the baker was not looking, and tried to keep himself warm by flapping his wings.

3 **watchman:** (Nacht-)Wächter.
18 **to glisten:** glänzen.
icicle: Eiszapfen.
19 **dagger:** Dolch.
eave: Dachrinne.
24 **crumb:** Krume.
26 **to flap one's wings:** mit den Flügln schlagen, flattern.

But at last he knew that he was going to die. He had just enough strength to fly up to the Prince's shoulder once more. "Good-bye, dear Prince!" he murmured, "will you let me kiss your hand?"

"I am glad that you are going to Egypt at last, little Swallow," said the Prince, "you have stayed too long here; but you must kiss me on the lips, for I love you."

"It is not to Egypt that I am going," said the Swallow. "I am going to the House of Death. Death is the brother of Sleep, is he not?"

And he kissed the Happy Prince on the lips, and fell down dead at his feet.

At that moment a curious crack sounded inside the statue, as if something had broken. The fact is that the leaden heart had snapped right in two. It certainly was a dreadfully hard frost.

Early the next morning the Mayor was walking in the square below in company with the Town Councillors. As they passed the column he looked up at the statue: "Dear me! how shabby the Happy Prince looks!" he said.

"How shabby, indeed!" cried the Town Councillors, who always agreed with the Mayor; and they went up to look at it.

"The ruby has fallen out of his sword, his eyes are gone, and he is golden no longer," said the Mayor; "in fact, he is little better than a beggar!"

"Little better than a beggar," said the Town Councillors.

15 **to snap:** (entzwei)brechen, zerspringen.
17 **Mayor:** Bürgermeister.
20 **shabby:** schäbig.

"And here is actually a dead bird at his feet!" continued the Mayor. "We must really issue a proclamation that birds are not to be allowed to die here." And the Town Clerk made a note of the suggestion.

So they pulled down the statue of the Happy Prince. "As he is no longer beautiful he is no longer useful," said the Art Professor at the University.

Then they melted the statue in a furnace, and the Mayor held a meeting of the Corporation to decide what was to be done with the metal. "We must have another statue, of course," he said, "and it shall be a statue of myself."

"Of myself," said each of the Town Councillors, and they quarrelled. When I last heard of them they were quarrelling still.

"What a strange thing!" said the overseer of the workmen at the foundry. "This broken lead heart will not melt in the furnace. We must throw it away." So they threw it on a dust-heap where the dead Swallow was also lying.

"Bring me the two most precious things in the city," said God to one of His Angels; and the Angel brought Him the leaden heart and the dead bird.

"You have rightly chosen," said God, "for in my garden of Paradise this little bird shall sing for evermore, and in my city of gold the Happy Prince shall praise me." CW 285–291

2f. **proclamation:** Bekanntmachung.
8 **furnace:** Schmelzofen.
16 **overseer:** Aufseher.
17 **foundry:** Gießerei.
19 **dust-heap:** Kehrrichthaufen.

Editorische Notiz

Die Texte werden nach folgenden Ausgaben unter Angabe der Sigle und Seitenzahl zitiert.

CW	*The Complete Works of Oscar Wilde*, hrsg. von Vyvyan Holland, London: Collins, ^{3}1992.
TL	*The Letters of Oscar Wilde*, hrsg. von Rupert Hart-Davis, London: Rupert Hart-Davis Ltd., ^{4}1963.
Tr	*The Trials of Oscar Wilde*, hrsg. von H. Montgomery Hyde, London/Edinburgh/Glasgow: William Hodge & Company, ^{2}1960.
WaH	*The Wit and Humour of Oscar Wilde*, hrsg. von Alvin Redman, New York: Dover, 1959.

Das Glossar erklärt in der Regel alle Wörter, die nicht in *Reclams Englischem Wörterbuch* von Dieter Hamblock (Stuttgart: Reclam, 1996) verzeichnet sind.

Im Glossar verwendete Abkürzungen

adv.	adverb
arch.	archaic (veraltet)
fig.	figuratively (übertragen)
Fr.	French
o.s.	oneself
pl.	plural
s.o.	someone
s.th.	something

Fremdsprachentexte

IN RECLAMS UNIVERSAL-BIBLIOTHEK

Englische Prosa

Margaret Atwood: *Polarities.* Selected Stories. 170 S. UB 9008

James M. Barrie: *Peter Pan.* 219 S. UB 9294

John Buchan: *The Thirty-Nine Steps.* 221 S. UB 9051

Anthony Burgess: *A Clockwork Orange.* 261 S. UB 9281

Lewis Carroll: *Alice's Adventures in Wonderland.* Ill. 165 S. UB 9160

Gilbert Keith Chesterton: *Two Father Brown Stories.* 80 S. UB 9223

Joseph Conrad: *Heart of Darkness.* 189 S. UB 9161

Roald Dahl: *Three Tales of the Unexpected.* 96 S. UB 9215 – *The Witches.* 192 S. UB 9080

Charles Dickens: *A Christmas Carol.* 155 S. UB 9150

Arthur Conan Doyle: *The Speckled Band.* Four Sherlock Holmes Stories. 184 S. UB 9003

Daphne Du Maurier: *The Birds.* 76 S. UB 9287 – *Don't Look Now.* 109 S. UB 9054

English Aphorisms. 148 S. UB 9296

Nadine Gordimer: *Town and Country Lovers. Three Stories.* 96 S. UB 9237

Graham Greene: *The Basement Room.* Selected Stories. 144 S. UB 9015 – *The Third Man.* 173 S. UB 9180

James Herriot: *Yorkshire Tales.* 165 S. UB 9044

Aldous Huxley: *Brave New World.* 323 S. UB 9284

Christopher Isherwood: *Goodbye to Berlin.* 328 S. UB 9010

James Joyce: *Dubliners.* A Selection. 104 S. UB 9181

Judith Kerr: *When Hitler Stole Pink Rabbit.* 268 S. UB 9076